HOW TO SUCCEED IN BUSINESS BY REALLY TRYING

Michael Hill

Avid Readers Publishing Group
Lakewood, California

The opinions expressed in this manuscript are those of the author and do not represent the thoughts or opinions of the publisher. The author warrants and represents that he has the legal right to publish or own all material in this book. If you find a discrepancy, contact the publisher at www.avidreaderspg.com.

How to Succeed in Business by Really Trying

All Rights Reserved

Copyright © 2014 Michael Hill

This book may not be transmitted, reproduced, or stored in part or in whole by any means without the express written consent of the publisher except for brief quotations in articles and reviews.

Avid Readers Publishing Group

http://www.avidreaderspg.com

Library of Congress Control Number: 2014934893

ISBN-13: 978-1-61286-214-9

Printed in the United States

TABLE OF CONTENTS

Table of Contents	iii
DEDICATION	viii
ACKNOWLEDGMENT	ix
INTRODUCTION	xi

Chapter 1: THE REASON FOR THIS BOOK	1
Inspiration, motivation and passion	3
Chapter 2: PRINCIPLES FOR SUCCESS	7
A great work ethic trumps intelligence	9
Having skin in the game	10
Motivate employees to maximize your profits	10
Benefits of a good reputation	13
Create win/win solutions	14
Lemons to lemonade	14
Sales	15
Stop your lying ways	15
Lying for the greater good	18
Machiavellian philosophy	19
Always be fair	19
Speak no evil	20
Reprimanding employees	21
Don't steal other people's time	22
Stand by your principles	22
Never lose your temper	22
Business ethics	23
Politics, Power, Corruption and Betrayal	25

Chapter 3: THINGS TO KNOW FOR SUCCESS   29

Control is better than confidence	31
Cash is king	32
When banks lend money	33
Is it your desire to succeed or your fear of failure?	35
Find cash wherever you can	36
Want to be a corporate officer?	36
Never close escrow until the bastards are out	41
Publicly versus privately held companies	42
Cooking the books	43
Never equate likability to honesty or honesty to fairness	45
Business is not a democracy	46
Perception is reality	46
It will not always be your way	49
There is a little genius in all of us	50
My philosophy of no partners	51
Never allow a labor union to come between you and your employees	54
Listen and think	56
Going on a job interview	59
Negotiating and contracts	61
Using humor to your advantage	65
Overcoming objections	69
Money at 100% interest rate	71
Checks and tests	74
Checks and balances	75
Don't let the bastards sue you	77
Money doesn't buy you happiness	78
Happiness is just a state of mind	79
Know what your employees want	81
The power of "thank you"	84
Never let your attorney make business decisions for you	85
Legal documents	85
Giving a deposition	86
A bad decision is better than no decision at all?	87
Ready, fire, aim	89

Giving a speech	89
Stress is a good thing?	92
Passion, leadership and salesmanship	93
Always question authority and "experts"	96
Statistics are more than just numbers	97
Pay raises	98
Know your limitations	99
Patents, trademarks and trade dress	100
To be successful, always plan ahead	101
Never call your customers pricks	103
The true character of a person	103
Don't take a percentage of the profits	104
Never set your own hours	105
Know-it-all's	106
Don't put all your eggs in one basket	106
What is experience?	107
Accounting	107
Depreciation expense	109
Finance	110

Chapter 4: AVOIDING ROADBLOCKS TO SUCCESS   113

Don't change jobs too often	115
Climbing the corporate ladder	115
"Come on in, the water is fine!"	116
Management contracts	117
A wolf in sheep's clothing	118
To hate or not to hate?	122
Know your prospective employer	123
Don't risk losing good employees	124
"Try" is one of the worst words ever	128
Keeping your promise	129
Take responsibility for your mistakes	130
Violation of confidence	130
Avoiding employee lawsuits	131
Never classify your friends by race, creed or religion	133

Chapter 5: PROVEN TECHNIQUES FOR SUCCESS — 135

Become a cheerleader	137
Thinking outside the box	138
Choosing the right business career path	151
How we see the problem sometimes is the problem	153
Time management	153
A fistful of dollars and peer pressure	155
Power of persuasion	156
Avoiding bankruptcy	157
The art of bouncing checks	159
You may not know it, but you have a poor memory	162
Lead by example	164
Don't prioritize your schedule	164
Meetings	165
The Rule of 72	167
Interviewing applicants is a listening process	168
How do you know that you are hiring the right person?	170
Don't hire married couples	173
You must know your numbers to forecast	174
Effective report writing	180
Price sensitivity	182
Conflicts of interest within your company	183
Pricing your products or services	184
Economy of scale	186
Vertical Integration	188
When your company gets sued	192
Class action lawsuits	194
Good work habits	196
Yes, we are all procrastinators	197
How to deal with negative talk	199
Salaried versus hourly employees	200
If you want someone to be your friend, then let them do you a favor	201
If you want something done, give it to a busy person	201
Putting your best foot forward	202
Learn to love your job	203

Never present problems without solutions	205
Before you fire them, give them a raise	205
Don't take "no" for an answer	206
Always have a plan B	208
"There is no limit to how far you can go, as long as you don't care who gets the credit"	209
Using e-mails as a great tool	210
Know when to shut up	210
Get a guarantee of performance	212
Don't kick the tires too hard	213

EPILOGUE 215

DEDICATION

This book is dedicated to the most influential person in my life, my mother, Jane (McGovern) Hill.

She was the second oldest of 10 children and the oldest daughter. At age 11, when the stock market crashed in 1929, her father lost his shoe manufacturing business in Logan, Ohio. She readily accepted the responsibility of helping raise her eight younger siblings during the Great Depression. Eminently qualified, she raised her own two children beginning at age 27. I can't imagine growing up without the nurturing hand of a loving mother, and for that I am eternally grateful.

ACKNOWLEDGMENT

Lynne, my wife, for her love, positive influence and unwavering support during my career, without which my extraordinary career and hence this book would not have been possible.

Trevor Miller, my oldest grandchild, for being an unwitting participant in my educational experiment and for validating the effectiveness of my teachings, which provided me with the inspiration, motivation and passion to write this book.

Pat Hill, my sister, for her encouragement and priceless feedback. She has always been the smart one in the family.

George Dietrich, my best friend for over 60 years since kindergarten, for his proof reading, editing and invaluable input that added greatly to this book. He taught me to be brief and to use the least number of commas (,) as possible, and I absolutely, positively, and without a doubt could not agree with him more on both issues, especially the one about eliminating commas, if at all possible, because, after all, the reader knows when to pause, and you certainly wouldn't want to have run-on sentences. (He obviously didn't edit this acknowledgment but surprisingly it actually passed Microsoft's Word grammar check!)

Uzzell Branson, a good friend and an accomplished attorney, for his editing skills and for giving this book its chapter structure.

George Jaramillo, a good friend, an attorney and consultant, for his insightful input and for allowing me to tell his story of Politics, Power, Corruption and Betrayal.

Dan Clark, a good friend, a fraternity brother and successful businessman, for his support and favorable input.

Robert Silverstein, a good friend and an accomplished attorney, for his editing and encouraging advice.

Alan Faiola, a long-time good friend and an extremely successful international businessman, for his generosity in having his illustrators create the book's cover.

Dominick Rubalcava, the most loyal of friends, a fraternity brother and my attorney, for his friendship and for always being there for me whenever I needed advice over the course of my entire career.

John Belcher, a good friend and an accomplished attorney, for numerous thought provoking brainstorming sessions and for his legal advice, which aided me greatly in both my personal life and business career.

Jerry Furrey, a teacher by trade and a wealthy philanthropist by nature, for his never ending support of absolutely everything that I attempted to accomplish in my career. He is the big brother that I never had and a man with a heart of gold. He would literally give you the shirt off his back. He and his wife Bobbie are two of the most generous and kindhearted people that I have had the pleasure to know. Their struggles to become extremely successful through dedication and hard work should be an inspiration to everyone and is a true example of the basic theme of this book.

To all of the above, and to all of those who were gracious enough to review this book, which included Brent Romney, Dr. E. Forrest Boyd, III, Alan Faiola and Thad Gembacz, for their unselfish giving of both their time and invaluable input, which has made this book far superior to what I could have accomplished on my own.

The following are the first two reviews that I received that gave me encouragement in the early stages of my manuscript so they deserve special thanks:

"Loved this read! Extremely well written with excellent examples to clarify points of discussion mixed with a number of hilarious quotes!" Arlene Deter

"An enjoyable read, very practical and amusing. It would be a wonderful mandatory reading for a lot of young people." Maureen Bright, co-founding partner of Bright and Brown law firm

INTRODUCTION

This is a book of how best to position yourself for success. It embraces an indispensable "value system", creative strategies and time tested techniques for success.

After forty years as a president or vice president of a half dozen companies, both privately and publicly owned, and having owned two businesses, I have been faced with a wide variety of interesting challenges. My specialty was in turning around troubled companies and in growing businesses very quickly through planning, organization and team building. The experiences and lessons learned have given me a number of core beliefs for success.

This book is not an autobiography, however, it does include numerous anecdotes of lessons learned and how I learned them to give you a frame of reference and insight into my perspective. Essentially, from a relatively young age I adopted a "value system", or a set of principles based on Judeo-Christian beliefs that included everything from being fair, honest and ethical to being tolerant, forgiving and taking responsibility for my actions. Your value system plus strategies and techniques discussed in this book will position you well for success in all stages of your career, from going on an interview and becoming an entry-level employee to becoming a manager and eventually the president of a company. It will be your ability to successfully combine your value system with the application of your accumulated knowledge (education and experience) that will ultimately determine your level of success.

As you will learn in the first chapter, this book was written for the sole benefit of my grandchildren. It was only after receiving both encouragement from family and then favorable reviews from a wide variety of successful business and professional people that I decided to have it published for the benefit of others.

Even though this book was written for those over 18, my objective was to write about a "value system" that could easily be understood by those as young as 13. There are, however, sections of the book that will be beyond the understanding of those who do not have a basic understanding of both algebra and accounting, which are the only two prerequisites to fully understand everything being presented.

CHAPTER 1

THE REASON FOR THIS BOOK

Michael Hill

INSPIRATION, MOTIVATION AND PASSION

It all started during the summer of 2005 when the owner/president of a company for which I had been a vice president for 10 years asked me to teach his daughter, a USC business school senior, my "value system for success". I was honored and viewed this as not only an awesome responsibility but also an interesting challenge, especially since she would be arriving in just two weeks. I quickly prepared an outline of 75 topics, which was subsequently expanded to over 130 for a great "summer school" session. I used my outline again five years later to teach my oldest grandson, Trevor.

In September of 2010 Trevor was starting his senior year in high school; so, with a little nudging from my wife, I decided it was none too soon to start preparing him for the real world of responsibility. Borrowing from my own experiences, I offered him a job of gardening with me for two hours per week. The overall unemployment rate in California at the time was over 12%, but among teenagers it was well over 25%. Since he knew from his friends that finding a job was almost impossible, he jumped at the opportunity.

What Trevor didn't know was that the task he was about to embark upon was much more than just gardening. To his pleasant surprise he was going to be paid for two hours but would only be required to actually work for an hour and a half. I paid him for the last half hour just to sit and listen to me talk. After six months we had covered everything that was in my original outline for this book.

On Trevor's first day he showed up for work wearing those dreaded loose fitting pants that only covered about half of his butt (the fashion of the day). After giving him some basic safety tips and removing his cell phone and I-pod headset, I set him off on the task of picking up piles of leaves. Watching him work was one of the most comical things that I have ever witnessed; I could hardly believe my eyes. As he bent over to pick up a handful of leaves, his pants would drop down below his butt. After placing a handful of leaves into the barrel he would stop, remove his gloves and pull up his pants. After putting his gloves back on he would repeat this process over and over again!

Since I had started Trevor at $10 per hour ($2 above the minimum wage) I explained that his "technique" was worth no more than $1 per hour; corrective action was immediately required. The new work rules required either a belt or proper fitting pants. He readily agreed; he didn't want to fail at his first job.

After a few weeks Trevor's productivity increased; however, he started arriving late and on one occasion was a no-show. This was a great opportunity to explain <u>that employees must show up for work and show up on time,</u> as an employer would give a tardy employee a verbal or written warning and place it in his or her personnel file. After several warnings an employee would either be fired or passed up for a raise or even a promotion. To Trevor's credit, he was neither late nor failed to show-up after that warning. Subsequently, as a reward for his improved efficiency and more responsible work ethic, I increased his pay to $20 per hour. He was becoming a great employee.

After several more months, I decided to "test" Trevor regarding one of my lessons of doing more than you are asked. At the end of the workday I strategically placed a small three-foot long branch on the pathway to the trash receptacles. Trevor had one more barrel to take to the receptacles so I went inside the house and explained to my wife and his mother the nature of the "test" and how I planned to give him a $10 bonus if he took the initiative to pick up the branch. The three of us anxiously watched through the window as he carried the last barrel of leaves. His mother laughed and said that it was a no-brainer that he couldn't possibly miss seeing the branch and would pick it up and place it in the trash. But he didn't; instead, he not only stepped over it going to the receptacles, but also on his way back to the house.

When I pointed out to Trevor what he had done, or rather not done, he said, "What branch?" He really wanted to do a good job and had been making great strides; he was genuinely embarrassed that he had not passed the "test". When I showed him the branch, he was totally mystified and swore that he had not seen it; he would have bet his life that it was not there. This turned out to be a great opportunity for a lesson about being aware of your surroundings and not simply being a robot going from place to place. In other words, I wanted him to be aware of his surroundings and to take appropriate action on his own initiative whenever he saw something that was out of place.

A year after Trevor began working for me a great job opportunity of sales assistant became available at Sport Chalet, a sporting goods store. There were 50 applicants but only 4 openings so Trevor knew that it would be a long shot securing one of those positions. To his credit he asked for my help. I not only reviewed my prior lesson on interviewing with him, but also staged a mock interview so that he could learn by going through the actual process. Almost any young person's first effort would have left a lot to be desired and Trevor was no exception. The following were the reasons why he fell short in the mock interview:

- He had poor eye contact.
- He hemmed and hawed when asked about his strengths.
- He was caught off guard and started laughing when asked about his weaknesses.
- When asked if he had any questions, he had none.
- He forgot my fictitious name when it was time to thank me for the interview.
- He never asked for the job.

These were all things that Trevor realized had to be corrected if he was going to get the job.

I am proud to say that Trevor learned his lesson well as he successfully secured one of those four positions. Trevor was one of four applicants interviewed at the same time; and, afterwards, he told me that he was ecstatic when the interviewer asked if anyone had any questions and no one spoke up affording him the opportunity to ask his prepared question; namely, "What is Sport

Chalet's 'mission statement'?" Trevor told me that the interviewer appeared impressed with his question and proceeded to define the term "mission statement" to the others and then recited Sports Chalet's "mission statement". (A "mission statement" is a written statement of a company's goals and reason for being in business, which it shares with its employees and customers alike.)

Now for my proudest moment, after his first year at Sports Chalet and while working with me in the yard Trevor said, "Grandpa, I want you to know that your lesson about being aware of my surroundings has become so natural to me that I don't even have to consciously think about it anymore; noticing things that are out of place has become a habit and taking appropriate action has become who I am." It was at that exact moment that I decided to turn my life's experiences into a book for the sole benefit of my two younger grandchildren.

Never had I imagined that I would ever write a book, however, seeing the positive effects of my teachings on Trevor gave me the inspiration, motivation and passion to document everything that is in this book.

Over the course of my career I have read a number of "how to", "self help" and business books for the purpose of learning as much as possible from those who had preceded me; however, none attempted to cover the broader spectrum of business. In the absence of such a book, I wanted to arm my youngest grandchildren, Zander and Logan, with the benefit of my accumulated knowledge in the event that I am not here to teach them. It is my hope and belief that this knowledge will prove valuable in your life as well.

CHAPTER 2

PRINCIPLES FOR SUCCESS

Michael Hill

A GREAT WORK ETHIC TRUMPS INTELLIGENCE

My Great Depression Era parents of the 1930's made a point of instilling a **great work ethic** in me at an early age, which is without a doubt the <u>most influential lesson of my life</u>. Additionally, since neither parent received a college degree, going to college was not something that I should do but rather something that I must do. My folks also made it clear that I would be responsible for paying 100% of my college education. Hence, by the age of 10 I was already saving money for college by mowing lawns with our family's push lawn mower.

After working for more than 40 years I have learned that a great work ethic trumps intelligence every time. Obviously, you need to have brains but I have seen countless "intelligent" people not live up to their potential, while a less intelligent person who works hard is extremely successful and often beats out the more intelligent, but less hard working competitor.

I have never been accused of being the sharpest pencil in the box, but there were few, if any, who worked harder (a good friend and competitor once joked that the epitaph on my gravestone should read, "I wish I had worked harder"). After you complete your formal education you will gain additional knowledge during your career, however, your basic intelligence level will remain a constant; so, the big variable is, you guessed it, hard work. Fortunately, for people like me there are plenty of opportunities out there, so make the best of it.

"Knowledge is knowing a tomato is a fruit. Wisdom is not putting it in a fruit salad." Anonymous

HAVING SKIN IN THE GAME

My next lesson was on my 12th birthday when my father made me an offer that I couldn't refuse. After earning money by mowing lawns with a push mower for two years he offered to buy me the best professional power lawn mower on the market, which not only had a power reel but also was self-propelled. However, I would have to pay 50% of the cost, or $75, which was a lot of money in 1958, especially for a 12-year-old. He said that he wanted me to have a vested interest in this investment. Since I figured that I would be able to at least triple my business I accepted the deal. This was the first time in my short life that I was in debt and even though I wasn't paying any interest I didn't like it and my dad knew it. Consequently, I suspended my college savings plan and paid him back within three months. Hereafter, having skin in the game guaranteed my father that I was totally committed to succeed.

MOTIVATE EMPLOYEES TO MAXIMIZE YOUR PROFITS

At age 13 I learned that in order to expand my lawn mowing business I had to solve the time consuming task of hand trimming (the weed-whacker would not be invented for another 25 years). I started hiring neighborhood kids and learned two valuable lessons; first, having employees allowed me to exponentially increase my own income; but second, I had to hire and train motivated individuals with a vested interest in our mutual success.

Not wanting to spend too much time making sure they were doing their work in a timely manner I paid them a fixed amount for each job (piecework) so they would have skin in the game. I loved paying by the job instead of by the hour because it rewarded the faster workers and I didn't get sand bagged by the slower ones. Quality work wasn't a problem since they didn't get paid until the customer paid me, and no one was going to pay for poor workmanship. I also learned that the faster I paid after the completion of each job the more my employees became motivated, unlike receiving a paycheck every two weeks, or receiving a monthly or annual bonus.

While in college I read a labor efficiency study that stated that a proper incentive could potentially increase productivity by 50%, hence the conclusion that **the average worker only works at 67% of his or her capacity.**

In retrospect, I had actually learned this lesson first hand at the age of 13. At that time I was charging $3 per hour for general yard work when one of my customers, Mr. White, asked how long I thought it would take to trim a 150-foot long massively overgrown hedge with manual hedge clippers. When I said that I didn't know he insisted that I venture a guess so I said about 40 hours. Based on my hourly rate that would translate to $120. He then offered me a deal, "I will give you $150 for the job even if you can do it for less than 50 hours." He went on to say, "If it takes you more than 50 hours, I will pay you your hourly rate of $3; you can't lose." I anxiously accepted the deal and quickly calculated that if I could do it in 30 hours I would be making $5 per hour!

Mr. White was a smart guy and I learned a very valuable lesson trimming his hedge. For the first 33 hours I really busted my butt; however, I realized that I was only 50% done with the job so I knew that I wouldn't be able to make more than my $3 per hour rate. Consequently, I lost my added incentive and shifted to my normal working speed. I completed the job in a total of 83 hours and was paid $249. Since I had completed the second half in 50 hours I figured that it had actually been a 100-hour job that would have paid $300. The incentive had motivated me to work 50% faster but only for the first half of the job. I didn't feel cheated as I felt that he was being very fair but he certainly got his money's worth and I ended up learning a valuable motivational lesson.

So how do you make use of the knowledge gained from the hedge-trimming story? Well, if we assume that a job takes an average worker 100 hours to complete, then we know that it would be possible to complete the job in as little as 67 hours with a proper incentive.

In retrospect, if Mr. White had known that the hedge job was a 100 hour job which would have cost him $300, then he could have offered to pay me $240 (80hrs x $3) for the job even if I was able to complete it in less than 80 hours. Since I could have completed it in 67 hours I would have made an extra $39 (13hrs x $3) and Mr. White would have saved $60 for a win/win incentive plan. Incentive plans that are set too tight never work because the reality of not being able to make the extra money will set in very quickly, just as it did with me.

As a cautionary note, incentive plans can be great; however, whenever the pace at which the job is being performed is increased, the quality of the work generally decreases. Being aware of this inverse relationship will allow you to establish strict quality control guidelines. Safety may also be an issue; great care must be exercised in deciding which jobs lend themselves to incentive plans.

As an additional cautionary note, incentive plans that are set too loose, or too easily achieved, can be a big problem as well. This is especially true for salespeople who start making "too much" money. I can't count the number of times that a disgruntled salesperson had told me that they had quit a job because they had been "penciled". If you are not familiar with this term, it means that a manager retroactively changes a pay plan, which has a resulting negative effect on an employee's compensation. As a manager or an executive don't put yourself in this position in the first place. You need to anticipate all possible outcomes of an incentive plan in advance; however, if you find that you must change a pay plan, use a scalpel and not a hatchet.

Some may say that by using incentives you are essentially taking advantage of or exploiting your employees, but I couldn't disagree more. Incentives are a big part of the success of capitalism as it creates a partnership whereby everyone benefits. Of course, those who put their capital at risk will benefit the most, but capitalism also provides gainful employment for others and is the best system in the world. Any failure of capitalism is not a failure of capitalism but rather a failure of government with its over-regulation and anti-capitalistic policies.

"Government's view of the economy could be summed up in a few short phrases: If it moves, tax it. If it keeps moving, regulate it. And if it stops moving, subsidize it." Ronald Reagan

BENEFITS OF A GOOD REPUTATION

As a young entrepreneur I found that producing dependable work was not only appreciated by my customers but also built my reputation as a hard working responsible individual. This in turn opened up new opportunities. When I was 14, Jim Stewart, a 74-year-old retired industrial hardware worker, who was one of my customers, was looking to hire someone to help him build his hobby of making pet cages into a business in his converted three-car garage. The cages were constructed of galvanized sheet metal and industrial wire cloth and he named the company Better Products Company. Jim was a great mentor and taught me to operate a lathe, milling machine, spot welder, shear, punch press and hand break. Despite the 60-year age difference, after two years at age 16 he offered to sell me half his business for $2,700, which represented less than half the cost of the company's depreciated assets in 1962. Even though this cash deal represented about half of my college savings I jumped at the opportunity. Since I still had two years remaining before graduating from high school there would be plenty of time to not only replenish my savings but also to earn more prior to and during college by working 15 to 20 hours per week. This certainly beat mowing lawns during hot summers and I could work at night after school during the week.

CREATE WIN/WIN SOLUTIONS

Little did I know at the time but my greatest challenge was just two short years away when my partner had a stroke and died. This would be my first lesson in "management in crisis" as Jim had not only performed half the labor but he also performed all of the sales, invoicing, payroll and purchasing functions. Talk about baptism by fire! I was ill prepared to handle this situation but by sheer necessity the first thing I did was to negotiate a buyout of his widow's half of the business while simultaneously executing a formal lease of her garage. This gave me great security and gave her immediate cash plus a continuing income. It was truly a win/win solution.

LEMONS TO LEMONADE

Even though I had managed to save enough money for college, the timing of Jim's death could not have been worse. I had just started attending the USC School of Engineering and shortly thereafter my father found himself unemployed for an entire year for the first time in his life. As it turned out, it was a blessing in disguise as I hired my dad to help in both production and sales while I concentrated on the hiring and training of six part-time high school students. I also simplified the manufacturing process by redesigning the products and by buying new equipment to eliminate a lot of the spot welding. This not only improved the quality but also reduced the labor cost. Additionally, I needed a new punch press die to go with my new designs but I didn't know where to have it made so I went to a local city college, Pasadena City College, and spoke to the shop teacher who agreed to make it a class project at little cost to me. Within two years we went from selling to a dozen pet stores to over 200 pet stores in three states through five distributors.

A saying that reflects a positive "can do attitude" is "**Lemons to lemonade**", which I fully subscribe to. During my

40-year career I learned that sometimes a solution to a problem often turned out to be so good that I wondered why it hadn't been thought of previously. Sometimes the best ideas only come to us out of necessity and the best ideas are only limited by our ability to think creatively.

"The significant problem that we face can not be solved with the same level of thinking that created them". Albert Einstein

SALES

There is a saying in business that "Nothing happens until someone sells something." Therefore, regardless of your particular area of expertise always keep in mind that the primary lifeblood of any company is its sales. Consequently, all decisions regarding your business must first take into account how it will affect your customers and your sales. This is what I call the <u>first principle of understanding business</u>.

Other topics pertaining to sales, such as passion, salesmanship, power of persuasion, pricing, price sensitivity, economy of scale, thinking outside the box and not taking "no" for an answer are all discussed later in this book.

STOP YOUR LYING WAYS

From a young age my mother taught me to never tell a lie, not only because doing so was wrong, but because I was not smart enough to get away with it. Of course, my adolescent response was, "So you think I am stupid, or what?" She explained that virtually no one is smart enough to lie and get away with it forever. Lies always have a way of catching up with you since a liar needs to constantly remember what lies he or she told and to whom. The truth is easy to remember as it is what you would have said in the past to anyone.

Not being as dumb as I looked (or so I thought), I wasn't going to just take her word for it, right? I obviously had to test out her theory on my own. Well, the opportunity would come none too soon when totally out of the blue she asked if I had been smoking cigarettes, which, of course, I flatly denied. After all, how could she possibly have known what I had done two hours before in my friend's garage while she was still at work; absolutely no way, impossible. I adamantly stuck to my guns until she offered me a full immunity deal (no such deal would have been possible with my dad who fortunately was still at work). She not only forgave me for lying but also rewarded me for confessing by saying that I could smoke at home anytime that I wanted when she was home as long as I promised not to smoke away from the house in public as it would reflect badly on her parenting skills. Wow, did she know how to ruin a good time or what? I never took her up on her offer, as that was my first and last disgusting cigarette; I absolutely hated it but who knew that someone could actually smell it on your breath? I guess I really did have a lot to learn.

For parents it is not always easy to get to the truth. As an example, when my two oldest grandchildren Trevor and Zander were 13 and 6 years old respectively they were playing in my yard and, as boys will do, they began throwing rocks into a small stream that runs through the property. Being naturally concerned about an escalation in their activity, I told them not to throw any rocks into our swimming pool. Well, about 20 minutes later I noticed what looked like small rocks at the bottom of the pool so I asked who did it but neither confessed.

Since Trevor was the oldest I told him that I was holding him responsible unless he told me the truth, at which he said, "I can't tell a lie, Grandpa, it was Zander" (very noble of him). Having heard that, Zander got extremely upset and very passionately said, "Honest Grandpa, I swear I didn't throw any rocks into your pool; it was dirt clods." The lesson that I learned was that the next time I would have to be a little more specific regarding my instructions!

You must build a reputation of being a person of integrity so that when a questionable situation arises in your life - and it inevitably will - you will be given the benefit of the doubt. In order to be believed you must have credibility but <u>you can't have credibility if you do not have integrity</u>. Being seen as a person of integrity is the highest level of trust and respect that one can attain and it can only be obtained over an extended period of time by being straightforward and honest in your daily dealings. Therefore, start practicing this good habit as early in life as possible as no one wants to be known as a person that can't be trusted.

Unfortunately, this may not be as easy as you think as we all learn to lie as early as two years old. Lying starts in an attempt to avoid blame and to get what we want as children. "Johnny, did you eat all of the cookies?" "No!" Lying is actually a demonstration of intelligence as it requires a certain amount of planning and consideration of how what you say will affect the end result. So when your child lies to you in their early years, they are just exercising their brain! A more credible or sophisticated lie would be, "No, Nicky did it", or possibly an even more plausible denial, "What cookies?" The bottom line is that everyone not only has the ability but also the tendency to lie; however, if you are not viewed as a person of integrity then you can forget about a successful business career. <u>Stop your lying ways as early in life as possible</u>. If you are already a person of integrity then protect it at all costs. If you sense that someone's perception of you is that you did something underhanded then you will need to confront that person and clear up any misconception as soon as possible. Being perceived as a person of integrity is one of the most important assets that you can possess in the business world because without it nothing else matters. Would you knowingly trust your money to anyone other than to a person of integrity?

"If you tell the truth, you don't have to remember anything."
Mark Twain

LYING FOR THE GREATER GOOD

Oops, just when I said not to lie! Well, I guess there are exceptions to every rule, like when your wife asks you if her jeans make her look fat! Comedian Jay Leno once said, "Why do they always try to blame it on their jeans? Wouldn't you just love to say that it isn't your jeans that make you look fat, it's your fat ass that makes you look fat!"

As a project manager for The Leisure Group one of my first projects was to move one of its 26 manufacturing operations throughout the U.S. and Canada from Monterey, California to Pine Bluff, Arkansas. I was told that this was a top-secret project and even the operations manager did not know about the move. Despite it being against my nature I was instructed to say that I was an efficiency expert and that my assignment from the corporate offices was to document standard costs and manufacturing procedures over a three-month time period. Not wanting to fail at my first job out of graduate school I learned that I was a better liar than I thought (mother would have been so proud). For my own mental health I learned to be a loner and kept from making friends at the plant, which minimized my conversations and the need to lie (you need to live in your own skin). I more than made up for the friendship deficiency by the overwhelming reception that I received from the good people in Arkansas.

The deception was necessary for the greater good of the company. On a more positive note, once the company announced its intentions to shut down the plant everyone received a 100% pay increase during the move and phase down process, which for the bulk of the employees lasted about three months; so, in a way I felt a little better about having lied.

This thinking is part of the Machiavellian philosophy of looking out for the greater good.

MACHIAVELLIAN PHILOSOPHY

During the middle ages Machiavelli, a philosopher and historian, held strongly to the belief that the opposition who had sworn allegiance to others could not be trusted to ever be loyal subjects. The lesson here is that you should never keep employees who are not loyal to you as they will not be loyal to your company. Disloyal employees are one of the worst problems for a company and are a cancer that must be removed. Not only are they disloyal but also their dissention can contaminate others and they will always be counter-productive to the company's goals. This type of employee will sabotage you by either trying to make your projects fail or not help make them succeed. And they will always be the first to blame you for the failure. A leopard never changes its spots so any hope that you may have that these employees will change for the better is misguided.

"Just because you're paranoid doesn't mean they're not out to get you!" Colin Sautar

ALWAYS BE FAIR

Being fair may seem blatantly obvious, but it is not always easy and should not be taken for granted. In fact, it is one of my highest priorities because it is the key to building respect and gaining trust and support, which is critical for developing a team spirit and fostering a team effort. A big part of being fair is sharing credit when credit is due. Reprimands are also necessary when needed and will allow a failing employee to take corrective action. It would be unfair to fire someone for poor performance if you have not first given them proper warning along the way.

A part of how others perceive you is by the **fairness** that you show in both hiring and promoting employees. By giving preferential treatment, or by showing favoritism, you will lose respect and demoralize the more deserving employees. Hiring or promoting family members is usually very problematic. Along that line, one of my employers was a little confused when he asked me if it is called "incest" when you hire a close relative. Well, I very respectfully informed him that the correct word would actually be "nepotism", unless however he was planning on having sex with them, in which case both words would be correct!

Great care must also be given in creating fair and equitable pay plans so as not to create inequities within your company. Pay is a relative thing; so, make sure that inequities in your pay scale policy are avoided at all costs. As an example, a manager making $60,000 per year may be very happy until he or she learns that the janitor is making $70,000!

Hard work and good job performance should always be rewarded in one way or another, even if it is just a pat on the back.

Always keep in mind that it is infinitely more important to be fair than generous, as <u>fairness is always respected</u>, but generosity is too often taken for granted. <u>One of the worst things that someone can say about you is that you are not fair</u>.

SPEAK NO EVIL

Whenever speaking about someone make a habit of visualizing that person in your presence. In other words, never say anything about a person that you would not say to his or her face. Make a habit of this and avoid the ugliness. Take the high road.

Have you ever had a good friend break up with someone and in your effort to comfort him or her you put-down the estranged person only to later learn that they got back together? Not only does your good friend, or possibly former friend, know what you think of his or her significant other, but his or her significant other will probably know as well. In comforting friends it is always best to just shut up and listen. They will probably do more than enough bashing on their own. Just be supportive by being a good listener, period.

We don't live in a vacuum and as we know from the police shows, "What you say can and will be used against you." Never participate in negative conversations about other employees, as it will always reflect badly on you. Instead, always be the one that points out their positive attributes. When it is their turn to be on the hot seat, they will know that you can be counted on to be fair and not jump on the bandwagon. What are your feelings towards a person who is bad mouthing someone else? Think about it. People usually don't see how ugly they are when they do this. Don't be that person.

REPRIMANDING EMPLOYEES

Reprimanding employees in front of others is a major mistake. Regardless of how egregious the problem, publicly demeaning or humiliating anyone gains nothing good. In fact, there is a lot to be lost; namely, a loss of respect for you from anyone that witnesses it, and a fear that they may be treated in the same manner in the future. This will lead to losing good employees or their faith and trust in you as being a fair and compassionate person. <u>Employees do not need to like you, but they do need to respect you in order for you to be an effective leader</u>.

Unfortunately, I lost an excellent accounting employee two months after she had witnessed her boss being chewed out in front of other employees by the president of the company. Despite my offering her a 40% pay increase to stay, she refused by saying, "I love my job and I would like to stay; but I know that someday he will yell at me and I will walk out. I won't be able to take it, and since I can't afford to be without a job, I have found another one which actually pays a little less than I am making now." Obviously, after she had witnessed his tirade she felt that her <u>job security was at risk</u>, which to her was absolutely everything.

DON'T STEAL OTHER PEOPLE'S TIME

People who are constantly late are usually disorganized and inconsiderate. You certainly do not want to give that impression. In fact, you should look at it the same way that you look at stealing something tangible. When you are late you are stealing the other person's time. I have actually met people who have told me that they felt a certain amount of importance by arriving late to a meeting............go figure! Don't let your ego get in the way of good common sense and good business practices.

"If you can't be on time, be early."   Vince Lombardi

STAND BY YOUR PRINCIPLES

Sometimes you will find that by standing firm on your principles you will actually benefit financially because the opposition will have a difficult time arguing against solid principles. This is especially true if you know that they share the same principles. Always remember that the best principle to stand on is fairness. Make your money and its return on investment a part of your principles.

"It's not just the principle, it's the principal plus the interest!" Anonymous

NEVER LOSE YOUR TEMPER

Losing your temper is an outward sign that you can't cope with the issue at hand. Temper stifles your creative problem solving abilities because your emotions take over. Always be in control regardless of how upsetting the situation may seem as there will always be an opportunity to come back to that issue after you have had a chance to properly reflect on it while in a calmer state of mind. Problem solving solutions come to us at the strangest times but rarely in the emotional heat of battle.

Having said that, I must say that I sometimes found it helpful to **act** like I was really upset and angry in response to what someone had said in order to make an emphatic point. Not being one to swear, I have unfortunately found that it was helpful to occasionally use a curse word, but never in real anger, in order to get someone's undivided attention while making a critical point. I have also found that by not being known as one who swears or raises his or her voice on a regular basis makes you much more effective when you do it sparingly. I do not condone the use of profanity; I am simply pointing out that I occasionally found it necessary (a sad commentary on either my lack of communication skills or on some uneducated subordinates, or possibly both).

I must point out that my mother would have totally disapproved of my use of curse words as she had taught me that vulgar language was not only uncouth but it also was a sign of your ignorance with a lack of a proper vocabulary. She believed that you should always be able to articulate what you want to communicate using civil language with an extensive vocabulary (unlike me, she obviously never supervised a crew of longshoremen).

"People who fly into a rage always make a bad landing."
Will Rogers

BUSINESS ETHICS

A reputation for being ethical and for being a person of integrity should be at the top of everyone's priority list of personal assets.

Most of the answers to ethical questions are pretty straightforward, but sometimes, and for some people, it is not so easy. Ethics is not always straightforward or obvious, and there are even ethics committees in law firms and in large corporations to deal with the more complex issues. Ethics can involve issues from conflicts of interest to insider stock trading and everything in-between. The issues can be complex, but for most of us, we simply need to follow our moral compass.

Once I was asked to present false documents to a bank in order to secure financing. I responded that it would be a fraud and that it would also be a federal offense as the banks are FDIC insured. I was then offered a written indemnification as an inducement. I immediately refused, period. Years later I learned from a defense attorney that you couldn't legally indemnify someone for committing an illegal act. Since I had refused the offer from the outset, I had never even thought about the legality of the indemnification at the time but in retrospect it is 100% obvious. A good example would be if someone asked you to be the getaway driver in a bank robbery, then a written indemnity from the gunman who ends up killing the bank teller will obviously not clear you of murder charges! There are people who have gone to prison who actually thought that they would be immune from prosecution just because someone convinced them that they would be "indemnified", or otherwise would not be a fall guy.

"If a customer overpays you $20, do you keep it or share it with your partner?" Anonymous

Obviously the answer is that you give it back to your customer. Your honesty will leave a big impression and your integrity will be rewarded with more business from a trusting customer.

POLITICS, POWER, CORRUPTION AND BETRAYAL

George Jaramillo, an attorney and consultant, worked for me as Vice President of Administration of Krystal Enterprises for three years and I helped prepare him to take over the operational portion of my duties prior to my retirement in 2009. Previously, at age 36, George had become the youngest Assistant Sheriff of Orange County, and reported directly to the Sheriff, Mike Corona. This was a position in which he was responsible for thousands of police officers under his command, and which he held for several years.

George is a brilliant individual. He is scary smart. Due to his law enforcement experience, after September 11, 2001 he was invited to the White House a number of times to help advise on national security issues during President Bush's administration. He also testified before congress on issues of homeland security.

When George was 5 years old his father was assassinated in South America; so, his mother left the country with her twin sons and moved to the United States. Jon Huntsman Sr., the billionaire owner and founder of Huntsman Industries, began mentoring George as a teenager. Huntsman is the world's largest supplier of polyurethane cups and packaging for McDonald's hamburgers. (Jon's son by the same name was the Ambassador to China and ran for President in 2012.) George received a great education and subsequently received a law degree by attending law school at night while working as a police officer during the day.

While attending a political fundraiser in Orange County George met Mike Corona and immediately struck up a friendship, which resulted in Mike running for Sheriff of Orange County with George's support with his law enforcement credentials. In 1996 Corona won the election and appointed George as Assistant Sheriff. Corona was re-elected for a second term in 2000, and campaigned partially on his belief in term limits as he said he was only going to be a two-term sheriff. He promised George that if George helped him get re-elected for a second term and remained to help him run the sheriff's department, then he would not run for a third term and would endorse George for sheriff when he stepped down. Corona had loftier ambitions at the state level but the 2004 political climate was not favorable for a state campaign.

Near the end of Mike's second term in 2004 George received a phone call from an internationally known sports star, whose identity George asked me to keep confidential. The sports star didn't want to speak over the phone so he asked to meet with George about a matter of great importance. At the meeting he informed George that Mike Corona was secretly making plans to run for a third term despite his promise to George. He admired George and didn't want to see him get blindsided. Besides, he was also aspiring to work in law enforcement himself and didn't like underhanded tactics.

When George confronted Mike and informed him that he would be running against him for sheriff, Mike said, "No you won't." He then told George that he was fired! Having been best friends for eight years and having done a great job of running the department, George was absolutely shocked, but this was just the beginning. In an effort to totally discredit him, Mike had George indicted on charges of misappropriation of public funds for the personal use of a sheriff's helicopter. Even though there were compelling reasons for the use of the helicopter and George had reimbursed the county for the $250 cost for a 12-minute flight, he pled no contest and was sentenced to eight months in a private jail. George had been working for me at Krystal for about six months at the time of his sentencing in March 2007 and he was a personal friend of the owner. A leave of absence was authorized, which I wholeheartedly supported as George was a very valuable employee and we had become very good friends.

It was a great day when George returned in December 2007, as I had missed his administrative expertise and engaging personality, but his problems were far from over.

Ever since the filing of rape charges against volunteer assistant sheriff Don Haidl's son, Greg, and subsequent allegations of a cover up by the sheriff's department in the case, the FBI had been investigating the sheriff's department for possible corruption.

Making a long story short, George cooperated through the corruption investigation against Corona. Corona was only convicted of witness tampering as he had been secretly recorded via a wiretap while speaking to Don Haidl regarding a plan to lie about monies that had exchanged hands. Corona was sentenced to 5-1/2 years in federal prison, which he started serving in Colorado in 2011.

    Unfortunately, in spite of George's cooperation, he received a 27-month sentence in federal prison for not reporting "minimal taxable income" and for corruption for allegedly not reporting gifts that he had received. After George finished serving his time in 2011, he was completely exonerated on the corruption charges. Essentially, the court decided that the acceptance of gifts by a public official was not corruption if nothing was given in return. In George's case, there were no allegations of anything being given or sought in return so there was no corruption.

    Additionally, George won his lawsuit against Orange County for his wrongful termination by Corona. Essentially, police officers have employment rights i.e. the right to have their case reviewed prior to termination. The judge ruled that his rights had been violated and awarded him nearly one million dollars.

    The many lessons learned here is that power can corrupt, politics can be dirty (usually is), and betrayal can be extremely costly.

Michael Hill

CHAPTER 3

THINGS TO KNOW FOR SUCCESS

Michael Hill

CONTROL IS BETTER THAN CONFIDENCE

You will obviously be more efficient if you delegate some of your work load; however, never forget that you are still ultimately responsible for its success or failure. Consequently, never delegate anything that you are not prepared to follow up on. Way too often things will **slip through the cracks** as the person that you delegated to may not share your work ethic or sense of priority. Since your employees can "make or break you", don't put your fate totally in their hands.

While Vice President of Operations of Vogue Coach I had assigned a task to our purchasing manager, Ed Hale, who unbeknownst to me, had subsequently delegated it to Dori, his lovely assistant. After about a month, I followed up with Ed only to find out that it had completely slipped through the cracks. I read him the riot act about allowing things to fall through the cracks that could have shut down the production line if I had not caught it. He knew that this was one of my pet peeves as I had fired his predecessor for the same reason. He said that he was sorry and that it would never happen again; he offered no excuses. An hour later, Dori came to my office looking very sheepish, and asked if she could speak with me. I said, "Fine, what's up." She very nervously said, "Mr. Hill, I just wanted you to know that it was not Ed's fault, as it was actually my crack that it slipped through!" No sooner were the words out of her mouth than she realized how it sounded. Well, we had a good laugh and I appreciated her honesty and no one was fired. Ed had been one of my first employees at Better Products Company; so, I already knew that he was extremely reliable and he turned out to be one of the best purchasing agents ever. In contrast, his predecessor had screwed up on a weekly basis and was absolutely incorrigible. This was during very stressful times when we were increasing production by 400% over a two-year period; keeping the production line supplied in a timely manner was absolutely critical.

As a good friend often said, "Control is better than confidence." Never assume that something important will be handled, or is being handled properly.

CASH IS KING

My first job out of graduate school was as a project manager for The Leisure Group. This was my first exposure to the operations of a successfully run public company, which was founded by two extremely bright Harvard MBA's, Steve Hinchliffe and Merle Banta.

The Leisure Group owned 26 leisure time manufacturing companies throughout Canada and the United States which included; Himalayan Backpacks, Sierra Bullets, High Standard Shot Guns, Lyman Telescopic Sights, Flexible Flyer Sleds, Blazon Swing Sets and Ben Pearson Archery to name just a few.

In its first five years the company was a textbook case for a successfully run business that had profitably doubled it's sales every year. The lion's share of its growth was through acquisitions and once it reached $30 million in sales they were faced with the prospect of acquiring a $30 million company in order to continue this rate of growth. Their acquisition target was Yardman Industries, a sit-down lawn mower manufacturer in Ohio, which was going through a business contraction with severe cash flow problems that were not identified during the due diligence period. This error almost took down an otherwise profitable organization. Had The Leisure Group not been so leveraged with its bank, the company's CEO would not have been able to play hardball to get the bank to lend more money, which ultimately saved the company. My surprising first hand lesson was that it was actually possible for even a profitable company to go bankrupt. No doubt about it, "Cash is King".

The hardball strategy that was implemented was the shutting down of all 26 manufacturing facilities, which included laying-off all of its employees, and then "giving the bank the keys to the business". After three days, the bank caved in and decided to protect its outstanding loans by lending the company even more money and the company was back in business. Unfortunately, the company became heavily burdened with debt, which eventually lead to its downfall. As a cautionary note, the bank loan saved the company, however, your objective should never be to become solvent through borrowed funds.

When a company has sufficient cash to pay its debts in a timely manner it is said to be "solvent". In contrast, a company that is unable to pay its debts when due is called "insolvent". An insolvent company cannot continue to operate, as it will be forced to close its doors by its creditors. **In order for any company to survive it must not only be profitable but also solvent.** As an example, a profitable company that has all of its cash tied up in other assets, like equipment and inventory, may very easily become insolvent and be forced to close its doors.

WHEN BANKS LEND MONEY

Banks are always willing to lend you money when you least need it, so don't get in trouble by borrowing to your credit limit just because you can. When you really do need money the banks may be very difficult to deal with in terms of increasing your line of credit or giving you favorable interest rates. You will also be required to sign a loan agreement, which will include the bank's "covenants". Covenants are like the 10 Commandments (i.e. the Ark of the Covenant, which is thought to have housed the 10 Commandments), however, in the bank's case they never limit themselves to just 10, and if you are in violation of any one of them, then you are in default of the loan agreement.

As an example, one of the covenants may require that you maintain a certain level of profitability each month, or be required to maintain certain ratios, like between your net worth and debt. In a privately owned company the banks will also require personal guarantees from the owners. The loan agreements are only for a specified period of time, which may not be renewed by the bank even if you are not in default.

There has been many a good company that had grown so fast that they borrowed themselves into trouble, and yes, the banks will foreclose on them. **<u>Your objective should be to operate your company debt free</u>**. Unfortunately for most companies, the banks continue to be a necessary evil. **Bad times never last, and neither do the good times; so, always plan for the bad times during the good times in order to be able to survive the bad time cycle. If you wait too long, it may be too late and I guarantee you that the bad times will come, as it is just a matter of time.**

During my 40-year career (1970 thru 2009) the **bad times** came a total of 7 times for an average of every 5-1/2 years as follows:

- **1973**: The first energy crisis
- **1979**: The second energy crisis
- **1980**: Prime interest rate of 21.5% and tight money credit
- **1987**: The stock market crash in October '87
- **1991**: The first Gulf war in Iraq
- **2001**: The World Trade Center attack of 9/11 and the subsequent start of the second Gulf war in Iraq
- **2008**: The Financial Melt Down on Wall Street and the beginning of the Great Recession.

Depending on the industry, these events could range from a mild to a major affect on a company. The industries hit the hardest were the oil-reliant industries, like the auto and recreational vehicle industries, and the financial industries, like the banks and investment companies.

"A bank is a place that will lend you money if you can prove that you don't need it." Bob Hope

IS IT YOUR DESIRE TO SUCCEED OR YOUR FEAR OF FAILURE?

What motivates you? Is it your desire to succeed or your fear of failure? In my experience most successful executives are driven by their fear of failure. Business is never a static situation and all executives will encounter both good and bad times in their career. What defines the success or failure of an executive is how he or she handles the tough times. For the successful executive, it is the fear of failure that is the greatest motivator because if you are not afraid to fail, then you are not committed to succeed. My fear of failure was so compelling that it almost consumed me in both time and thought; but, regardless of whether I succeeded or failed, it has always been my motivating factor. The toll that it takes on your life can be extremely damaging but the challenges and occasional successes always kept me coming back.

During the bad times I had to control the stress that comes with the fear of failure, or else I would not have survived. Every Sunday night at 6 PM, like clockwork, I would start getting a nauseating headache, but I never understood why until years later when I reflected on my career and how I had survived some very stressful times. Well, what I realized was that during the work week I never had a headache as I was way too busy solving problems, which kept both my body and mind busy actively interacting with people and solving problems. The adrenalin rush or endorphins that were released from this challenging activity was absolutely exhilarating. I then realized that my problem on Sunday nights was that I started planning my next day's activities. The anticipation of what I was going to do and the possible outcomes consumed my thinking but there was no adrenalin rush or endorphins being released because I was not able to put anything into action until the next day; so, the frustration over the inactivity resulted in my stress related nauseating headaches. In retrospect, I should have occupied my time in the gym, which I subsequently ended up doing later in my career. Exercising and being physically tired not only helped shut down my brain but it also guaranteed me a good night's sleep.

Fortunately, I eventually learned this (I was just disappointed that it took me so long).

FIND CASH WHEREVER YOU CAN

As President of Executive Industries, a turnaround company, I learned to conserve cash by selling its operating facilities in the high rent district and relocating the company to a lower rent district for a cash flow savings advantage. Additionally, I found cash by selling non-performing assets like Huffaker Engineering, a wholly owned subsidiary. Huffaker Engineering manufactured racecars for NASCAR racers, the most notable of whom was none other than the legendary Dale Earnhardt. Unfortunately, after the 1979 energy crisis, none of the auto companies were sponsoring racecars. One sponsor, Super Cuts, was barely keeping the company from losing money; the immediate prospects did not look good, as there was no positive cash flow. The proceeds from the Huffaker sale were critical to Executive's survival. Furthermore, since Executive Industries had not been profitable for two years prior to my arrival we could not afford to carry a faltering subsidiary in the event that its business did not soon improve. I hated to part with that company, but it was absolutely the right thing to do at that time.

WANT TO BE A CORPORATE OFFICER?

Wow, how cool would it be to be an officer of a corporation! Well, the pay increase is great; and the power, the responsibility and the authority are awesome, but be aware of the potential downside. As an officer of a corporation you are exposed to unpaid tax liabilities. I mention this above all other liabilities because of the number of times that I was hired to turn around cash poor companies. In a corporation, which is an entity in its own right, officers generally have protection against lawsuits from both creditors and customers unless they are successful in "piercing the corporate veil". Basically, someone can recover damages from you personally as an officer of a corporation if you willfully commit a fraudulent act or fail to treat the corporation as a separate entity from yourself. These usually involve either committing fraud against someone or commingling corporate assets with your own. Personal integrity and walking the straight and narrow will **usually** protect you from these types of exposure.

The most common exposure of an officer is the liability of not paying payroll taxes. I have seen a number of struggling companies that have kept its doors open by using the cash from unpaid payroll tax liabilities. It starts out simply enough by thinking that it will only be one time to get over a rough spot until business picks up; but it is extremely dangerous and even a bankruptcy filing will not absolve you of this debt to the IRS. Don't fall into this trap as it can ruin your life. Unpaid unemployment taxes also falls into this category. The only difference is that the Employment Development Department (EDD) collects unemployment taxes. If you think the IRS is difficult to deal with, wait until you try dealing with the EDD. It will track you down at home and at work and hound you for life! Don't get me wrong; I am not trying to scare you out of becoming an officer but rather trying to scare you out of being tempted to play a fool's game.

If you were thinking that I am overly passionate about this tax issue because I played this fool's game, you would be wrong. My passion comes from my first hand experience of being unfairly targeted by the EDD. A year after closing down and liquidating a vehicle manufacturing company, the EDD came after me personally for what it said were unpaid unemployment taxes. Despite my denial, the EDD hounded me at home and at work with phone calls and letters. "Just pay what you owe" they would say, which was followed every month with a demand letter showing that my liability was increasing by 5% per month due to penalties and interest charges. I knew that the taxes had been paid because I had personally seen to it prior to the company's liquidation. Consequently, I consulted with an attorney and learned the only way the EDD could prevail in its case against me would be if it could prove that I "willfully" decided not to pay the taxes. A "willful act" means that I knew of the tax liability and disregarded my obligation to pay.

I decided to hang my hat on the fact that my only willful act was in actually paying the taxes. I successfully tracked down the former accounting manager and payroll clerk and had them sign a sworn statement stating that I had instructed them to pay all of the taxes and that all of the taxes had, in fact, been paid. I then scheduled a meeting with the EDD director and, without my attorney present, pleaded my case openly and honestly and vowed to fight them for however long it took regardless of the cost. I knew that I could stand firm on it not being a willful act even if the taxes somehow had not been paid. I didn't have my attorney present because it was not a complex issue and more importantly I wanted them to know that they would not be able to pressure me by running up my legal costs as I could very easily represent myself.

Three weeks after my face to face meeting I received a phone call from a very cheerful lower level EDD employee who said, "Good news Mr. Hill, this is your lucky day as the EDD has decided not to pursue its case against you since it would not be worth it." It would not be worth it? This could not be possible as we are talking about $50,000 nearly 25 years ago and I most certainly didn't scare anyone to death even though I would like to think so. It is my firm belief that the EDD discovered that it had made an error but of course would not admit to it or apologize. So, it was actually the acquisition of excellent legal advice in an area of the law about which I wasn't knowledgeable that ultimately led to my dispute with the EDD being resolved. Knowledge really is power.

A year after the closure of that business a customer from Illinois sued me personally. The vehicle he purchased two years prior for $175,000 had a defect, which could have very easily been corrected at a cost to the company of less than $500. Six months prior to closing the company I had been trying to convince him to allow the company to affect the repairs, however he simply wanted his money back and was being extremely stubborn. I suspected that he was having financial problems. I offered to fly a factory mechanic to his local dealer to affect the repairs at no cost to him. He finally agreed to have the repairs performed but he wanted the company to insure his vehicle as he had let his insurance policy lapse. I told him that I didn't have the ability to insure a vehicle that the company didn't own but that I would reimburse him the cost of the insurance for the week that the vehicle would be in transit to and from the dealership. I was shocked that he refused my offer and it was now clear that he didn't want his vehicle repaired. He was simply stonewalling the negotiations in a feeble attempt to have the company repurchase his vehicle under the Lemon Law. His repurchase request under the Lemon Law was totally unreasonable since the law only requires a manufacturer to repurchase a vehicle if the manufacturer fails to resolve a problem after three attempts. In our case we had not even been allowed one attempt.

After six months the negotiations came to an impasse at which time I proceeded to liquidate the company. Despite the liquidation, I kept my offer on the table to repair his vehicle since it was not only an inexpensive repair but also because it was simply the right thing to do.

Unfortunately, in his attempt to get his way he had his attorney sue me personally. This was the first and only time that I have ever been sued. When your company gets sued it is one thing; when you personally get sued it is quite another not only because of the stress but because of the legal cost of defending yourself with your hard earned after tax dollars. A company would pay these costs with <u>before tax</u> dollars, about half the cost that an individual would pay on an <u>after tax</u> basis. (All corporate expenses are deducted from income before calculating the profit; so, expenses are tax deductible prior to any taxes being paid; hence, all corporate expenses are paid with before tax dollars.)

In an attempt to pierce the corporate veil the plaintiff's attorney sued me for $500,000 in a Chicago, Illinois Federal Court under RICO (Racketeer Influenced and Corrupt Organizations Act), which was a law specifically designed to bring organized Mafia crime bosses to justice. It certainly was enough to ruin my day, to say the very least!

Lawsuits often take on a life all of its own. It includes numerous interrogatories, requests for the presentment of documents, depositions and numerous court filings. Interrogatories are a series of written questions posed by each side as part of the discovery process in the hope of discovering the truth. This process along with the scheduling of court hearings and conferences lasted a little over a year at which time my attorney finally was able to depose the plaintiff. At a deposition the opposing attorney is given the opportunity to question the person being deposed for the purpose of getting to the truth.

Fortunately, despite being stubborn, the plaintiff was an honest guy, so during his deposition he told the truth about how I had negotiated with him in good faith, which totally exonerated me of all charges. He also stated that he had never read the complaint that his attorney had filed against me. The judge in the case was so outraged by the false allegations made against me that he sanctioned the plaintiff's attorney and threw out the case. The sanctions essentially forced the plaintiff's attorney to either reimburse me for my legal costs or face the legal consequences in a court of law. Not only was I reimbursed for my legal fees but the judge also ordered the court records to reflect that all of the allegations made against me were found to be totally false. He said that he did this to keep the false allegations from reflecting badly on my character in the event that I ever decided to run for public office. Keep in mind that all court records are subject to public scrutiny.

We have the best judicial system in the world; however, I believe that we should adopt the English system of law whereby the loser pays for all legal fees and court costs for both parties. This would keep frivolous lawsuits from being filed in the first place. In my case, I was reimbursed for my legal fees not from the plaintiff but rather from his attorney and only because of the judge's sanctions.

As a final note, most healthy companies have both D&O insurance (Directors and Officer's liability insurance) and corporate by-laws that indemnify Directors and Officers against lawsuits. I mentioned "healthy companies" for a reason, as most financially troubled companies don't have D&O insurance; and, if a company were to go bankrupt, the company's indemnification would be meaningless since there would be no money to defend you. In any event, before becoming an officer of a company read their corporate by-laws regarding officer's liability protection and also inquire about D&O insurance coverage, especially if it is a financially troubled company.

NEVER CLOSE ESCROW UNTIL THE BASTARDS ARE OUT

While at Executive Industries I learned a valuable lesson during the relocation of the company's operating facilities. After negotiating the sale of the company's facilities and the purchase of its new facilities I was very careful to allow an ample amount of time to physically move our entire manufacturing operations, which I estimated would only take 30 days. The seller of our new facility had asked to rent back the facility for three months after the close of escrow and I agreed because we still had an easy 90 days to make the move and their rental cost was automatically deducted from the purchase price in escrow. Both escrows were successfully closed on time.

When the time came for the seller to move out they were in such dire financial straights that they could not afford to move and we are talking about 125,000 square feet of stuff in two buildings! Well, since they were in chapter 11, I had to deal with a hard-nosed court appointed SOB as opposed to the gentlemen with whom I had built a relationship. Every deadline was missed and they were still there two months past their original move out date and I needed to vacate our sold buildings within 30 days. I was at my wit's end since we needed a minimum of 30 days to make the move. Well, I met with the court appointed administrator and suggested that I purchase enough of their equipment to allow them to have the money to make their move and I also ended up helping them move out as we moved in. We made it under the deadline by two days but this was totally my fault for not foreseeing the possibility of this situation and it was a lesson learned that wouldn't soon be forgotten. Unfortunately, 22 years later a similar situation occurred to an experienced colleague, so beware, the bastards are still alive and well!

PUBLICLY VERSUS PRIVATELY HELD COMPANIES

In a publicly held company the objective is to maximize shareholder's worth, primarily by maximizing profits, which drives the stock price. Some public companies will "force profits" by whatever means possible. Whether they do it through creative accounting techniques or sales gimmicks, the bottom line is usually the same; namely, they end up paying higher taxes on inflated earnings. Also, they usually suffer from both cash flow problems, and a lack of future sales by pre-selling their products. Since you are only as good as your last quarterly profits this process continues quarter after quarter in an endless cycle of chasing your tail so to speak. This process gets more difficult with each passing quarter, so it really is a fool's game. The Leisure Group fell prey to this practice in three ways. Firstly, because the company was such a sales/marketing driven company, they maximized sales by pre-selling their products at the end of each quarter, which made it more difficult to sell their products in subsequent quarters since the demand had been saturated. Secondly, in order to pre-sell their products they gave 90 to 180 day payment terms, which created major cash flow problems. Lastly, by maximizing their profits, or "forcing their profits" for the benefit of their shareholder's stock price, they paid higher corporate income taxes. Hence, a perfect storm for disaster!

In a privately held company the objective is also to maximize profits, but never by inflating it whereby the company pays more income taxes. In fact, some privately held companies will try to understate its profits by using creative accounting techniques, like accelerated depreciation schedules, in order to save on income taxes and hence improve its net cash position.

During times of corporate losses some public companies will try to minimize its losses out of fear that its stock price will fall. On the other hand, some privately held companies will try to magnify its losses in order to create a larger tax refund since it doesn't answer to public shareholders.

Generally speaking, some publicly held companies have a tendency to be short sighted, whereas most privately held companies tend to operate a little more sanely. The exception, and there are always exceptions, is if a privately owned company is planning to go public or to be acquired by another company, in which case it will want to show the maximum amount of profits for the benefit of a higher selling price.

COOKING THE BOOKS

Why do some companies artificially increase its profits? How does it benefit them? Well, one company did this so that it would not be in violation of the profitability covenant of its bank's loan agreement, which would have resulted in the bank foreclosing on its loan. Other reasons that companies do this is to increase the company's stock price, which not only benefits the top management who may have a substantial ownership positions but also the company could benefit from a higher stock price if it decided to have a secondary stock offering by selling more shares to the public.

A public company that manufactured buses had inflated its profits by overvaluing its used-buses, which it had taken in on trade. As an example, it would sell a new bus for $80,000 and in return it would receive $50,000 in cash plus a used-bus valued at $30,000. This sale would generate an estimated profit margin of 10%, or $8,000. Okay, now enter the head book cooker who recorded the sale as a $100,000 sale in return for $50,000 in cash plus a $50,000 used-bus. Recording the sale in this manner increased its profits by

$20,000, so instead of an $8,000 profit margin it actually booked a whopping $28,000 profit margin. The $30,000 bus was put on the books for $20,000 over its actual value.

This is a fool's game and the company eventually filed for bankruptcy. One of its salesmen related this story to me and said that the downfall of this scheme was that it was impossible for them to sell a $30,000 used-bus for $50,000. Consequently, none of the used-bus inventory was ever sold and eventually their used-buses tied up all of the company's working capital, which amounted to over $2,000,000 in cash. The dilemma was that if they sold a used-bus for its $30,000 market value then they would incur a $20,000 loss on the sale, so they simply kept the used-buses in inventory at its inflated value.

In this case it was difficult to prove that management had actually perpetuated a fraud, so the bankruptcy court concluded that it was just poor management and no one was prosecuted.

As another example, a vehicle manufacturer cooked its books and bilked GE Financial out of $2,000,000 for the purpose of staying in business during extremely difficult times.

When vehicles are manufactured the manufacturer creates a title, which is called a MSO (Manufacturer's Source of Origin). It is this title that their retail dealers present to the DMV (Department of Motor Vehicles) after the vehicle is sold to a retail customer. The DMV then converts the MSO to a new title of ownership (pink slip), which is given to the retail customer.

This vehicle manufacturer was in deep financial trouble, so instead of just manufacturing vehicles it diversified its business by manufacturing bogus MSO's as well. It recorded on its books that it had manufactured these bogus vehicles that didn't exist and presented phony MSO's to GE Financial as collateral for a loan.

When GE Financial reviewed the company's books it appeared that it was a rock solid enterprise. The company masked its losses by showing a nice profit on the bogus vehicles that it placed on its books as an asset. With absolutely zero manufacturing costs on these bogus vehicles it was a very nice profit indeed!

GE Financial would lend 50% of the wholesale value on these types of vehicles. The manufacturer's vehicles had an average wholesale value of $200,000, so it "created" 20 bogus vehicles over the course of a two-year period that were valued at a total of $4,000,000 and borrowed a grand total of $2,000,000.

Since an average of 10 vehicles didn't exist at any given time, whenever the GE inventory guy showed up at the factory to verify the vehicle inventory he was told that those vehicles were at trade shows across the country. The manufacturer had about 100 total units in inventory, so the missing units didn't immediately raise any flags. The scam worked for about two years until the bogus vehicle count reached a grand total of 20 vehicles, at which time GE decided to fly agents around the country to verify the vehicles reported as being at shows. The company filed for bankruptcy protection and GE sued the owner for fraud.

The sadist part of this story is that the owner allowed his 30-year-old daughter, who was the Chief Financial Officer, to be the fall guy. She told the court that she was 100% responsible and that her father was completely unaware of her activities. They were counting on the court to be more lenient on a female, and maybe it was, but she still received a 5-year prison sentence.

NEVER EQUATE LIKABILITY TO HONESTY OR HONESTY TO FAIRNESS

Don't confuse a likeable person for an honest person. The best cons in the world are seemingly charming and likeable people because that is how they gain the confidence of their mark. Remember that it takes time to qualify someone as a person of integrity; so don't be too quick to trust someone you like. It is an extremely easy mistake to make and that is why con artists are so successful. Unfortunately, way too many people <u>equate being nice to being honest.</u> How many times have we heard a victim on the nightly news say "But he was such a nice young man"? **<u>This lesson is far too often forgotten so don't forget it. It could be the biggest mistake of your life.</u>**

Additionally, <u>don't equate honesty to fairness</u>. Sometimes honest people can be very greedy, so watch out. Later in this book I will give you specific examples of both of these beliefs and how I got duped.

BUSINESS IS NOT A DEMOCRACY

Business is a dictatorship, but it should be run as if it were a democracy of shared ideas; however, make it clear that after a decision is made, everyone must support that decision regardless of their personal beliefs. When you make a controversial decision, you do not owe anyone an explanation. However, I have learned that it is well worth the extra time and effort to make sure that everyone who was involved in the decision making process understands that you have additional confidential knowledge or other considerations that are affecting your decision but that their input was greatly appreciated. Keep in mind that others do not see everything that you see. Furthermore, it is important that they respect you and that they are enthusiastically willing to participate in future projects.

PERCEPTION IS REALITY

A person's perception **is** his or her reality; so, great care must be taken to understand how employees perceive decisions or changes within the company. Sometimes misunderstandings occur because of poor communications, or because of beliefs that are not true. Also, a person's perception may be filled with misinformation; but the bottom line is that **<u>a person's perception is 100% of his or her reality</u>** regardless of how wrong it may be. Misunderstandings can destroy a company; so, take the time to understand the beliefs that support people's reality. From their perspective, they are 100% right; and, in a company of 500 employees, there may be as many as 500 people with their own different view of reality.

It is extremely important, especially during difficult times, not to overlook the little things, which could lead to a negative environment within your company. This relates to the need to project a positive attitude and to understand that perception is reality.

I would have been totally ignorant of these truths had it not been for several loyal employees who enlightened me early in my career. I will share two examples of how I learned these lessons.

As the president of a turnaround company during very stressful times I would regularly walk through the manufacturing facility on a daily basis. I found this to be very therapeutic while I contemplated solutions to the company's problems. It was kind of like getting the cobwebs out of my head so to speak.

Fortunately, one of my loyal employees came to my office and told me that every time I would walk through the facility our factory workers would get depressed! Say what? The bottom line was that I had been unwittingly projecting a negative impression due to a facial expression of a concerned state of mind. This in turn created a perception in our employees' mind of eminent doom!

I immediately took corrective action by reminding myself to smile on my daily tours. Even though I had not previously been in a bad mood, I found that my smiles were reflected in the facial expressions of our employees, which had a favorable effect on me as well.

As I am writing this I am reminded of one of my high school teachers who on the first day of class introduced himself and then said, "You may have heard rumors that I am very moody; so, I just wanted you to know that there is absolutely no truth to those rumors. I am in a bad mood all of the time."

My other experience was with our office personnel. Because I wanted to create an atmosphere of being approachable, I had an "open door" policy both figuratively and literally; I very rarely closed my door. I quickly learned that whenever I did close my door the office rumors of the company's pending demise flourished.

What I learned was that, unless you keep your office door closed all of the time, closing your door occasionally signaled something of great confidential importance. The paranoia spread very quickly. As a consequence, I avoided closing my door and instead adjourned to other venues, like to our conference room or an empty lower level employee's office. Since everyone knew that my door was always open, I would jokingly say, "I have an open door closed minded policy." I found that relieving anxiety during difficult times was critical to focusing everyone on the objective at hand.

While I was a vice president of a company it was a defendant in a class action lawsuit involving an allegation of collusion and restraint of trade. In order to protect the company and to prove its innocence it was critical to garner the support of the industry's trade magazine publisher; so, the company's president sent the publisher an e-mail to solicit his support. Even though his response seemed to be supportive, he signed it "**cya,** Rick." In a panic, the president summoned me to his office while he dialed Rick on his speakerphone. I reached his office just in time to hear him scream, "What the hell do you mean by '**cover your ass**'!" Well, there was a long pause and then Rick very calmly said, "It means See Ya (cya)". The president was way too upset to see the irony but I laughed my ass off. In the end we were successful in proving our innocence and were subsequently dropped from the lawsuit.

E-mail is not the same as conversation, which is easy to misread, take out of context, document stupid remarks, etc. Incidentally, that's why lawyers love it. Nonetheless, even though conversation may be less confusing it is not always so. Our plant manager, Dominick, wanted his 7-year old son, Brandon, to be able to say what city he was from in the event that he ever got lost. He told his son that they lived in **Yorba Linda**, and then asked him to repeat it and he said, "my Balinda." Dominick was puzzled so he asked him again and Brandon just repeated, "my Balinda." Very patiently and slowly Dominick said, "No son, we live in **Y-o-r**-b-a Linda." To which Brandon said, "Yes Dad, just like you said, we live in **My** Balinda." Dominick then said, "Son, we don't live in **My** Balinda." To which his son said, "Yes, I know Dad, because you already told me that we live in **My** Balinda." Who's on first? You just have to love them!

As you can clearly see, everyone's perception is his or her reality and our sensory perceptions take a variety of forms. Therefore, great care must be taken, not only in the clarity of our verbal and written communications, but also in our expressions and actions, which can easily be misinterpreted.

IT WILL NOT ALWAYS BE YOUR WAY

When your supervisor makes a decision that is contrary to your point of view it is your obligation to the company to make sure that you do everything you can to make your supervisor's decision succeed. Don't let their decision fail due to your action or inaction, but rather set your personal feeling aside and support it whole-heartedly. By doing this you will become known as a loyal person that takes direction well. The whole is greater than the sum of its parts, so being known as a team player, despite your personal beliefs, will serve you well. If you believe in your point of view enough, then you will find a way to persuade your supervisor of your convictions; otherwise, either your point of view isn't such a great idea after all, or you need to work on your power of persuasion. **The best mindset for success at any level in a company is for you to become the employee that you would like working for you.**

I actually learned this lesson from one of my best employees, Gilbert, who was totally against one of my production plans as he thought it was way too aggressive, and he was right. However, his loyalty and extraordinary efforts to see my plan succeed was rewarded by 25 years of employment with me at three subsequent companies. Without his extra efforts my plan would not have succeeded; so, always remember the old saying, "your employees can make or break you", it is true.

What we accomplished at Vogue Coach was a 400% increase in production in just two years. This achievement required Gilbert to work with me until midnight on many occasions in order to cure production bottlenecks so that the next day's production would not shut down. Our success in not once shutting down production was a tremendous reward for both of us and solidified an enduring friendship.

THERE IS A LITTLE GENIUS IN ALL OF US

Have you ever noticed that some of the most successful people in life seem to be a little different? When I say "different" I mean that they seem to be a little strange and may even march to the beat of a different drummer! Some may be certifiably crazy, while others may be just scary smart in their area of expertise. I am convinced that everyone has a little bit of genius in them; but, most don't display it due to a lack of either initiative, confidence, motivation, or a failure to even recognize their own special talent. Your objective is to find what you are passionate about and discover your own special genius. Effective managers will also find and then utilize these talents in others, while compensating for any shortcomings.

It would be irresponsible and even dangerous if you ignore their shortcomings, especially with those who have severe deficits in either people skills or judgment. By compensating I mean making allowances, adjustments or accommodations to ensure that those individuals do not get into a position where he or she may be incompetent. This may prove to be very difficult, as egos are fragile and you may even risk a loss of respect from other employees who may think that you are not a good judge of character.

I don't know why I seem to bond with eccentric individuals, but I believe it is because I see the genius in them and they appreciate my recognition of their talent. For the most part, it has been extremely beneficial for my career. Interestingly, I have not only accepted them but also frequently embraced them as close friends. Sometimes my friends think I'm the crazy one, go figure!

Take, for example, Gilbert. His genius was in his leadership and organizational skills not to mention his dedication to hard work. He was also bilingual, which in southern California was a great asset with its high percentage of Hispanic factory workers. Oh, by the way did I mention that Gilbert could neither read nor write?

I once encouraged him to learn to read by telling him that if he could read he might very well become an excellent attorney. Later in life Gilbert was diagnosed with dyslexia, which answered a lot of questions, as he was far from stupid. He obviously counteracted his disability by becoming super organized and by being an extremely dedicated and loyal employee.

It has been my experience that the truly creative or innovative individual can very often be obnoxious, egotistical, impatient and intolerant. As a consequent, they may have a difficult time being hired, and if hired they usually don't work well with others and are regarded as being anti-social. Many will go their own way and start a company that sometimes becomes very successful, especially if they are smart enough to get out of the way of those better suited to running their company. Being supportive of these creative innovators will allow you to get the most from them.

MY PHILOSOPHY OF NO PARTNERS

In the late1970's I was introduced to Ed Mathews who I immediately sensed was one of those individuals with a genius level of talent for manufacturing fiberglass products. He was the sole proprietor of a fiberglass manufacturing company. Well, two years later he asked if I would be interested in investing in his company because he was desperate for additional working capital to grow his business. Despite a few warnings from some mutual friends about Ed's eccentric personality I agreed to invest. I was not interested in being a minority owner in a privately held company; so, we formed MTC Corporation with each holding a 50% interest. As additional security and as a savings to the company, I kept the books and generated monthly financial statements at night at no cost to the company.

Ed was a very interesting and talented guy. He had manufactured a number of fiberglass Mercedes front ends for the movie, "The Betsy"; he helped MATCO (Walt Disney's fiberglass company) solve fiberglass problems with some of their boat rides; and, he built race car bodies for Don "The Snake" Prudhomme, who was a legend in the sport of drag racing. Ed was also quite quirky, his boat was named "Dog Breath" and his college art project involved convincing a coed to sit in a mud puddle. He then poured plaster into the impression, made a plug, a mold, and then an award winning fiberglass piece of art which he titled "Buns In The Sun"!

Since I worked on the books at night, I usually spent some "quality time" with him prior to his leaving for home. As an example of our "quality time", on one typical night he grabbed my pencil and asked me to stop what I was doing and started asking me off the wall questions, like "What is the size of an elephant's belly button?" When I gave up and asked him what the answer was, he said with a big smile and in a very condescending tone of voice, "How the hell would I know that?" He then picked up the phone and called Night Owl, which was the Los Angeles Library's information nightline and asked them the question. They were stumped; but were equally fascinated as to why he needed to know; and, of course, Ed told them that he wanted to manufacture fiberglass belly button covers for elephants! Later that evening we figured that it had to be about 3 to 4 inches in diameter but fortunately production never got off the ground!

Despite our excellent personal relationship, a very strange thing happened. Eight months after relocating to a larger facility, the company had doubled its business and was making about five times its previous profits. I had foreseen this based on my analysis of the fixed and variable overhead costs relative to the potential for increased sales. After all, that was the reason why he needed the working capital and the reason why I had made the investment in the first place. Unfortunately, after informing him of the record setting profits, he disappeared for two full weeks and even his wife said that she had no idea of where he had gone. Essentially, he had abandoned the business and its customers who were becoming extremely irate due to missed deliveries.

After he returned he confided in me that he was incapable of sharing 50% of the profits with me, even though he had a nice base salary and I had none. <u>The bottom line was that he could not reconcile the fact that he was busting his butt, and even though he was making about twice what he had previously been making, he didn't feel that it was fair that I would be sharing handsomely on his efforts.</u> Yes, I had made a great investment, but from his perspective he had made a terrible deal.

I told him that he should have spoken up sooner and not risked ruining the business. Based on my perception of the damage to the company already, I proceeded to negotiate an amicable unwinding of our partnership. Three months later I was made completely whole on my investment and he received 100% ownership of the company but with very little working capital. Unfortunately, almost a year to the date after going our separate ways he filed for chapter 7 bankruptcy (a liquidation of the company). I believe that the damage that he had caused was greater than he thought, as no company will tolerate an unreliable supplier.

There is a saying in business that a percent of something is worth more than 100% of nothing. It's true.

Some of the most successful companies have had their origins with partners who possessed complimentary skills or separate areas of expertise. Unfortunately, just like my experience, I have seen far too many failures. Just like in the relationship in a marriage, which unfortunately ends in a divorce over 50% of the time, partnerships may start out great with the best of intentions but not only do circumstances change over time but sometimes the true person shows themself to be different than first thought.

Since everyone's perception is his or her reality, it is human nature to perceive things from our own sense of fairness. There will always be an evaluation of the other person's value relative to our own. I don't know that I would call it greed as much as a sense of fairness from our perspective; that is why we have marriage counselors. In other words, how would you equate a 50/50 partnership whereby one partner works 60 hours per week managing the business to maximize profits while the other partner only works 30 hours and plays golf twice a week, but generates 90% of the sales? Even if you can rationalize the equality, your partner may not.

I mentioned marriage, so I feel compelled to state that marriage is not a 50/50 relationship, but rather a 100/100 relationship in a successful marriage. Either you or your spouse may be at zero on some days, so the other partner must be at 100%. I must confess that I have been close to zero on some days, which I can't say about my wife, at least not in writing, but a committed partner will not allow the relationship to fail; after-all it is for better or for worse, so make the best of it.

NEVER ALLOW A LABOR UNION TO COME BETWEEN YOU AND YOUR EMPLOYEES

In the early 1900's unions served a valuable purpose by looking out for employee's rights regarding working hours, safety, working conditions, and compensation for injured workers. However, with the advent of numerous government laws, which regulate everything from safety (OSHA) and minimum wages to worker's complaints (NLRB) and worker's compensation for injured workers, unions are no longer relevant. Unions are counter productive for businesses as they add nothing to the product or services and are always trying to justify their value to their dues paying members by threatening a strike if the company doesn't give in to their never ending demands. Fortunately, unions have been losing their foothold on businesses as they have gone from representing almost 35% to less than 7% of businesses in the United States over the past 50 years.

Keep your company non-union by treating your employees fairly and as **individuals**. Never give the union an opportunity or a reason to represent your employees. The biggest difference between non-union and union employees is **individual treatment versus collective bargaining**. Make sure that your company has a comprehensive employee manual, which includes grievance procedures and a whole host of policies from raises to terminations. Never underestimate the value of good employee relations. **Include everyone** in all company-sponsored events. Don't create a policy of exclusion whereby the hourly employees are excluded from the company's Christmas party, for example, with only the salaried employees in attendance. **You need to maintain a company of inclusion and not one of exclusion if you want to keep the union out**.

Unfortunately, I had to learn this valuable lesson the hard way. While Vice President of Operations of Vogue Coach the company was blindsided by the UAW (United Auto Workers) as it had secretly signed up enough employees to force an election without management even knowing it. Since we were caught off guard, we were ill prepared for an election within 30-days and we lost by a large margin. The year was 1977 and the UAW representatives lied to the company's employees by promising them all of the benefits that the UAW factory workers were enjoying at the GM assembly plant in Van Nuys, California located about 15 miles from our facility. Our employees believed all of the UAW promises; but, when it came time for the UAW to deliver on its promises, it failed miserably. Within about 6 months the UAW called for a strike in an attempt to get what it was demanding.

The company's relationship with the UAW was always contentious. For example, whenever the union presented me with its grievances they were written in Spanish, despite my repeated requests for them to be submitted in English. Consequently, one day I decided to make my point in a way that would be guaranteed to get their attention. I dictated the company's response to my secretary and she wrote it down in short hand; but, instead of having her type up the response, I asked for her short hand notes and submitted those directly to the union. Well, until the strike, all grievances after that day were submitted to me in English.

When negotiations had broken down with the UAW and the employees had gone out on strike the company notified all of its employees in writing that unless they returned to work within 30 days they would be permanently replaced. Taking this type of action is not an uncommon practice during a strike as there is a business to run. As a result, all of the employees who had gone out on strike and not returned within 30 days, which amounted to about 250 of the company's 300 employees, were permanently replaced. The union eventually walked away after being on strike for a little over a year.

What I learned from this experience was that unions have a tremendous advantage in that it can promise anything and everything to employees with impunity; a company on the other hand is restricted as to what it can say. A company couldn't say, for example, that it would shut down or move the company if the union was voted in; however, the company could tell its employees about what happened at other companies, like how the union called for a strike at Vogue Coach and everyone that had gone out on strike lost their jobs. A company could also tell its employees that the union can't guarantee them anything and that they could actually be subject to a decrease in pay during the collective bargaining negotiations plus they would be required to pay union dues.

Twenty-two years later that experience helped me keep the union out of Krystal Enterprises with its 800 employees; yet another lesson learned that ended up paying dividends.

LISTEN AND THINK

After the UAW had called for a strike at Vogue Coach it filed 16 complaints against the company for allegedly violating labor laws. Each charge was extensively investigated by the NLRB (National Labor Relations Board) and 15 of the 16 charges were eventually found to be without merit and were dismissed; however, the one remaining complaint was deemed to have merit, so we proceeded to a NLRB hearing before a Federal Administrative Law Judge in a downtown Los Angeles courtroom.

It was a very stressful situation as the UAW had alleged that the company had increased the pay for most of its employees who had not gone out on strike, which would be an illegal inducement for them not to join the strikers. The stakes could not have been higher because if the union won the case then the court could force the company to rehire all of the strikers with back pay. And what would the company do with all of the replacement employees that it had hired?

I represented the company at the hearing and was flanked by two of the best labor attorneys we could find. As is common in high-risk cases, the attorneys instructed me not to speak and said that they would respond to all of the judge's questions.

For almost an hour the company's attorneys focused on justifying the raises given to the non-striking employees. After all, that was what the hearing was all about. Yet half way through their arguments I sensed that the judge was a little frustrated when he said, "But what about the striking employees?" They either didn't hear him or didn't understand what he meant, so they just simply continued to make their well-planned arguments.

The attorneys actually did a really nice job of explaining in great detail how the raises were either due to specific promotions or annual reviews; however, when they were finished it was obvious that the judge was not buying it when he said, "I am not finding your arguments to be very comprehensive or compelling because not a single striker was offered a raise; so before I rule in this case is there anything else that either of you would like to say?"

There was a long pause as I waited for one of the attorneys to say something, but when neither spoke up, I asked the judge if it would be okay if I said something. I could see that he was somewhat surprised that I had spoken up since I had just sat there for well over an hour without saying a single word. He probably thought that I was a potted plant! In a very nice tone of voice he addressed me directly and said, "Yes, absolutely". Since it was obvious that we had already lost the case, neither attorney voiced an objection.

The thought racing through my mind was why would we possibly want to offer the strikers a raise since they had been disrupting our business and harassing our employees every day while they crossed the picket line for almost a year. There was a tremendous amount of animus with a lot of name-calling and cars being scratched. It had become so bad that the police had stationed several officers at the entry to our business for months on end.

Needless to say, I was extremely frustrated with the prospect of losing this case and being forced to rehire these bad apples, and with back pay. The UAW had already cost the company several hundred thousand dollars in the disruption of its business and in the cost of defending itself against all of the union's baseless allegations.

This was, without a doubt, the scariest point in my career up to that point; so, I very quickly composed myself and focused my thoughts on the judge's stated concerns and addressed him by saying, "Your Honor, there actually were a number of striking employees who were, in fact, **eligible** for their annual review; however, I didn't have to call an attorney to know that I couldn't go out to the picket line and tell them that in addition to the company's last offer on the bargaining table that they would also receive a raise per the company's annual review policy. Doing this would obviously be considered an illegal inducement and I knew it." After a short pause, I then said, "Your Honor, what would you have done if you were in my place?"

Well, the judge flashed me a big smile and while still looking directly at me said, "I am prepared to make my ruling now and I rule in favor of the company. You will receive my written ruling within the next two weeks. Case dismissed."

What I learned was that being forced to be quiet made me a better listener, but whether you are forced or not, being a good listener will always afford you an opportunity to be a better thinker. Unfortunately, many people focus too much on what they want to say at the expense of not hearing everything that is being said. Again, the better the listener, the better the thinker.

In all fairness to the company's attorneys, I now feel that the judge was completely out of line in raising the issue of the striking employees not receiving a raise. The issue, and the only issue, should have been the justification for the raises for the employees that had not gone out on strike since that was the basis of the complaint. The attorneys should have objected to his line of thinking but they were either totally caught off guard, or possibly thought that it would be disrespectful to question the judge's line of thinking. Fortunately, not being totally versed on the law, I saw it as a legitimate argument that needed to be addressed.

We were so happy to have won the case that we simply walked out of the courtroom and went our separate ways without any further discussion; however, in retrospect I firmly believe that our attorneys fought the good fight and would have won on appeal had the judge ruled against the company.

Keep in mind that the striking employees had been permanently replaced, so not only were they no longer employees of the company, but their only possible re-employment and pay increase option was through the UAW at the bargaining table. Also, since the UAW represented the entire collective bargaining unit (all of the striking employees), the company was prohibited by law from taking any unilateral action like giving individual annual review raises to the strikers. If the company were to do this, it would be viewed as an illegal inducement in an attempt to entice individual strikers to return to work.

GOING ON A JOB INTERVIEW

After having interviewed hundreds of job applicants I have found that an alarming number of them were not prepared in the least. I have interviewed candidates for everything from janitor to president; so, I believe that I have seen the best as well as the worst interviews possible. Some things are basic in any interview, which many have either forgotten or have never known in the first place. I believe that the following are among the most important aspects of an interview:

Know as much about the company and the position as you can before you go on the interview. If possible, find out what you can about the interviewer, as this may give you some insight as to how to position yourself in terms of your questions or comments.

When you are introduced to the person conducting the interview, make sure that you commit their name to memory. This is critical, as everyone wants to feel like they are important enough that you remember their name. This is especially important at the conclusion of the interview when you thank him or her by name for their time and interest. Using their name during the interview is a good memory technique.

Make sure to make eye contact during the entire interview and listen carefully to the questions that are asked; you do not want them to have to repeat themselves, leaving the impression that you are not paying attention. However, having said that, if you don't clearly understand a question, then by all means ask them to qualify the question; you certainly wouldn't want to provide an answer that fails to address the question.

When asked if you have any questions about the company or job, don't do what a lot of candidates do and say nothing. Show some interest in the company and the position, but never ask questions about vacation time, hours or benefits, as there will be plenty of time to learn about this if you are presented with a job offer. Going into the interview you should already know the basic hours and general benefits; don't feel like you need to ask a lot of questions for the benefit of just asking questions.

Keep in mind that for most positions a company is interested in filling that position for a number of years, so don't be too aggressive in asking about promotions; an appropriate inquiry on the other hand would be to ask what opportunities have been presented in the past for employees entering at that position. I would also ask why the vacancy exists which will give you an idea if someone was promoted from that position, quit or was fired. If they had been fired, it would be natural to ask why which could give you incredible insight as to what not to do in that position and how fair the employer was in taking that action.

If asked about your strengths, be prepared to be as articulate as possible which will convey a sense of confidence in yourself and your ability to be articulate.

If asked about your weaknesses, be prepared and don't hem and haw; give a straight answer. The best answer that I ever heard was that they didn't feel they had any weaknesses except possibly for public speaking to large groups, which just about everyone can identify with. However, if you do have a weakness that may prevent you from doing the job, then by all means be honest and straightforward. This has happened in several of my interviews and I actually had to reassure them that it would not be a problem as we would take the time to train them, and I also thanked them for their honesty.

If at the end of the interview you are still interested in the position, make sure to **ask for the job**. This may seem obvious, but I have seen way too many candidates simply say "thank you" and walk out. The interviewer needs to know that you really want the job.

"I thought I wanted a career, turns out I just wanted paychecks." Anonymous

NEGOTIATING AND CONTRACTS

Always use the "house" when negotiating. In other words, never represent yourself as having the final authority in a binding agreement. In fact, by using words like, "It sounds reasonable to me, but I know that the owner will have a major problem with it due to his or her principles" will get you off the hook of being perceived as unreasonable. This will allow the negotiations to continue in a more agreeable fashion. It also buys you time to consider issues that you are not prepared to discuss at that particular moment, or which you may want to discuss with others first.

When a stalemate is reached during negotiations, there will always be a lull in the conversation as each side is posturing; and,

"the next person that speaks will end up losing". Regardless of how long the silence, never speak first, because inevitably, the person that speaks first will offer more or will give concessions in an effort to put the deal together. Even if the silence is deafening, let it just sit there.

The first that I had heard of this saying was 35 years ago from my good friend Karen Rentzsch, who had unwittingly benefited from it while on vacation in France. She had asked a French merchant how much an item cost and he gave her the price in francs. Well, while she was converting francs to dollars in her head, he got nervous and gave her a lower price. She once again began to convert it to dollars in her head, but before she finished, he once again lowered the price even further! She was prepared to pay the initial price quoted and had no intention of negotiating as she was not sure if it would be culturally correct; but, his nerves got the best of him during the long silence. In retrospect, she realized how it must have looked to the Frenchman, a woman doing mathematical calculations in her head telegraphing a facial expression of a contemplative state of mind with a slight hint of consternation! The poor guy never had a chance against this highly sophisticated American negotiator!

It is part of human nature to want to say something due to the uncomfortable atmosphere; so, you will need <u>to consciously remind yourself</u> that you will lose if you speak next; then, you will get through it. It is very tempting to speak after just a few seconds of silence, which will always seem longer. By keeping silent, you will not let them know what you are thinking, as opposed to opening your mouth and letting your thoughts roll out.

As President of Apollo Motor Homes, a turnaround company, and with a free hand to do whatever was necessary, I first proceeded to unload Apollo's non-performing assets. This included a very favorable 12-year master lease of a 110,000 square foot building that Apollo had vacated in order to downsize its operations. Fortunately, Grumman, an aerospace company, needed a building of that size to set up a repair facility to fix their subsidiary's buses. Grumman owned Flexible Buses based in Columbus, Ohio, and had designed a state of the art bus for Flexible with an innovative "A" frame chassis. The new design provided for a superior ride; however, all of its buses nationwide started to experience cracking of the "A" frames and engine cradles. One of the managers told me that this "A" frame failure was a major black eye for Grumman, and with tongue in cheek said, "I guess this advanced design would have worked well in outer space, but it was no match for pot holes and bad drivers here on earth."

Acting on Grumman's urgent situation, I made a call and hopped on the next flight from Los Angeles to Columbus in an effort to convince them to allow our company to affect the needed repairs. Upon my arrival, I received a tour of its massive production facility; and I found out as much as I could from my tour guide, including the fact that it actually employed 250 industrial engineers! A meeting was set up for the next morning, so I spent most of that evening preparing for my presentation. Since I would most likely be dealing with an industrial engineering manager, along with the fact that I have an industrial engineering degree myself, I felt very comfortable in presenting my proposal in terms that I knew they would understand, and hopefully embrace.

The next morning I met with Bob Coil, Flexible's Plant Manager, and four of his top managers. In 1980 Apollo's labor rate for non-union welders was $7 per hour. With aerospace union welder rates of about $20 per hour, I quoted a rate of $28 per hour, even though my bottom line number was $18. I knew that they would have to pay rent if they were to do the repairs themselves; so, I figured this would be a good deal for them as well. Bob immediately balked and asked me to give him a reduced price, but I told him that it was not worth our time to do it for anything less. I certainly was not going to negotiate against myself; the ball was in his court. There was a long pause; I knew that the next person that spoke would lose; so, I bit my tongue and shut up. It was an agonizing and awkward period of time, which seemed like an eternity but I said nothing. It is human nature to say something when one feels uncomfortable and sure enough Bob started rationalizing out loud about how it was still probably in their best interest to agree to my terms, which included being paid weekly for all man-hours worked. I learned first hand that the next person to speak really does lose.

If an agreement is to be drafted, don't take the lazy approach, but rather volunteer to draft the agreement. I have learned that this helps you in three ways: you control the time frame in which the agreement is drafted; you will be able to include everything that you want from the get-go; and, it will eliminate the possibility that you misread something if it is their draft since their choice of words may have more than one meaning.

One of the most important principles in negotiations is that of honesty; so always use tough-minded honesty in your business dealings. No one wants to do business with someone they perceive as not being honest.

When drafting any contract there are a number of obvious critical components. A good friend informed me of an error that he had made when signing an agreement with two sales reps that sold his products as distributors. They had exclusive marketing rights to sell my friend's products back east, but there was a critical component missing from the contract. There was no term; it was an open-ended agreement that would go into perpetuity! Well, after about five years the relationship deteriorated and my friend fired them, however, he ultimately lost a costly court battle. I don't know if I would have ever made this type of mistake; but, since it was such a costly mistake for my friend, I never forgot it. This is just another reason to draft your own agreements as I have actually been presented with contracts to sign that were open-ended but not obviously so. And of course, it also demonstrates the truth in an old but valuable lesson: <u>Always read the fine print.</u>

USING HUMOR TO YOUR ADVANTAGE

It has been my observation that the best negotiators and public speakers are those who use humor to their advantage. They use their humor to endear themself to others, thereby establishing a personal relationship. People will always look forward to meeting with them again as they are drawn to them. Winning people over with humor takes practice but it is something that can be very easy and will set the tone for a meeting or friendly negotiations. It usually requires a self-effacing comment, a little wit or a good-natured ribbing of others in an affectionate self-evident statement, like assigning a clever nickname. Never take yourself too seriously. People will always agree with your shortcomings, so that will always be a winner.

The following are a few examples of how others have injected a little humor into their lives:

I had introduced the company's attorney, George Jaramillo, at a meeting and when he was subsequently asked what kind of attorney he was he said, "A damn good one". Likewise, Manny Wolf, the Chairman of Allied Artists, a major motion picture company, never failed to get a laugh when he affectionately introduced me at meetings as his "token gentile".

Mark Willis was CEO of General Mills, the breakfast cereal company, and had been hired to become the CEO for Times Mirror. He was tasked with turning-around The Los Angeles Times, as they needed a hatchet man to drastically cut its overhead. He was my next-door neighbor for several years and told me that, due to his overhead cutting expertise at General Mills, he had been affectionately dubbed "The Cereal Killer".

Years ago I read about a motivational speaker who had an interesting ice-breaking introduction to his presentation. He introduced himself by saying, " Good morning, I am Bob Hoar, and that is spelled B.O.B."

During a neighborhood watch meeting, an NRA instructor said that a cop stopped an 84-year old woman and while checking her I.D. he noticed that she had a permit to carry a concealed weapon. He asked to see the gun so she showed it to him. He then asked if she had any other guns and she said yes in the glove compartment, so he asked to see it and she complied. He asked if that was it and she said that she had one more under her seat. The cop was amazed and asked, "Lady, what are you afraid of?" and she replied, "Absolutely nothing".

A motivational speaker at an engineering conference started his presentation by saying, "To the optimist, the glass is half-full. To the pessimist, the glass is half-empty. To the engineer, the glass is twice as big as it needs to be!"

In an introduction to a supply & demand economics class a professor told a story of a lady who had gone to her local butcher shop to buy ground beef and the conversation went like this:

Lady: "How much is your ground beef?"
Butcher: "Today's price is $4.50 per pound."
Lady: "That's outrageous; Joe's Butcher Shop across town only charges $3 per pound."
Butcher: "Then why don't you buy your ground beef from Joe's?"
Lady: "Well, he is out of ground beef today."
Butcher: "Oh, when we are out of ground beef we only charge $3.00 per pound as well, so why don't you come back tomorrow afternoon."

In my first accounting class at USC we had a very outgoing teacher, Mr. Caldwell, and for an accountant that was somewhat surprising to me. Everyone just loved this guy. I wish that I could remember all of his jokes as each one related to the subject matter. One that I will never forget is about a very old, but extremely successful accounting manager who was very mysterious. Every morning for years he would go to his office, unlock his desk and open the center drawer. He would then very quickly peek inside, slam it shut and lock it again. Well, after he passed away his employees could hardly wait to pry open his desk drawer to discover the secret to his success. To everyone's surprise there was but one small piece of paper that had been glued to the bottom of the drawer which read, "Debits to the left and Credits to the right". If you have not taken your first accounting class then you will need to reread this afterwards in order to fully appreciate this humor (or not).

    Russ Noles was an extremely vivacious engineer who worked for me in the motor home industry during the 1970's. He was known for never being at a loss for words and for always being the one to get in the last word. He had a great personality, which was based on his dry sense of humor and quick wit. Everyone enjoyed being around him and working with him.

    Being an engineer he decided to lend his hand to a new motor home interior design, which had been designed by the famed Ian Phillips, a premier home interior designer in Sherman Oaks. Ian had designed a rustic interior for one of our motor homes using leather sofas and chairs adorned with antique nail heads. Russ liked the design, but the company's standard brushed aluminum wall clock looked out of place. Consequently, he covered the clock with matching leather and used antique nail heads in place of the numbers. It was the icing on the cake. Everyone at the plant loved it, but what would Ian think? Russ was bubbling with pride and could hardly wait to see what Ian thought.

    Well, Ian loved it so much that he asked Russ if he wanted to be an interior decorator. Russ broke out laughing hysterically at the idea and said, "Do I have to be gay to be an interior decorator?" at which Ian immediately replied, "I don't know, do you want to be?" This was the first and only time that I ever saw Russ absolutely speechless. Instead of saying a word, he gave his best Jack Benny impersonation, pivoted 180 degrees and simply walked away. Everyone busted a gut laughing. Okay, it may not have sounded that funny, but like a lot of humorous things; you just had to be there to fully appreciate the humor. For those unfamiliar with the penny pinching Jack Benny, his expression was absolutely priceless as he pondered an absurd choice, like when he was seriously deciding what to do when a robber pointed a gun at him and offered him the choice, "Your money or your life?"

A Japanese businessman was giving a speech in the United States and started off by explaining the cultural differences between the two countries, "In Japan we always begin our speeches with an apology, whereas I have just learned that your custom is to begin with a joke. Consequently, I must apologize for not having a joke."

I was on a winter flight from Colorado to Las Vegas when the stewardess made the following announcement over the PA system:

"Since we have a sold out flight, please remove all of your clothes (a long pause) from the seat next to you." (It was a fun flight)

In justification for neurosurgeons making the kind of money that they command, despite what may seem to be a relatively short period of time in surgery, the head of neurology told his audience the following story: One afternoon while Picasso was having lunch at an outside cafe he began to draw a picture on his napkin, which did not go unnoticed by a lady sitting at the next table who was very impressed. After paying her check she approached him and offered to pay him whatever he thought his drawing was worth. After a moment of reflection he said $10,000, at which the lady let out with a scream of outrage and said, "But it only took you

30 minutes to make that drawing", at which he said, "No, you're mistaken Madame, it actually took me 40 years to draw this."

While attending a special forum in which Four Star Brigadier General Stanley McChrystal was the honored speaker, he told us an inspiring story of his life's accomplishments in the military, which was extremely impressive to say the very least. So as not to appear too braggadocios and also to endear himself to the audience, when he got to the part of his story where he was on stage with his wife, Anne, as he was being honored as a Brigadier General he said, "I was so very proud of myself, standing on that stage with Anne by my side with the band playing and all of the surrounding pomp and circumstance, that I leaned over to Anne and asked her if she had ever in her wildest dreams imagined standing on stage with a Brigadier General." Her response was priceless, "Stanley, you are not in my wildest dreams."

Obviously your personality will set you apart from the crowd. If you possess this ability, then people will eagerly seek you out. Your sense of humor will increase your likability and help ensure that people will listen to what you have to say.

OVERCOMING OBJECTIONS

In negotiations always be honest but don't be stupid by saying absolutely everything that you know. Your strengths will most likely be apparent however your weaknesses will probably also be known, so whenever possible try to use your weaknesses to your advantage. This is always risky as they may not be completely aware of any or all of your weaknesses, so be careful not to volunteer too many specifics. On the other hand, your honest straightforwardness may be very disarming and gain you credibility in other areas that they may have previously had doubts.

As an example, before the Grumman agreement could be finalized I had to learn how to overcome three objections of Grumman's Chairman, John Bierwirth:

1) How could a cash poor company whose parent company was in bankruptcy possibly perform on a contract?
2) How could we possibly hire upwards of 200 welders in a month?
3) On a personal note he somewhat sheepishly confided in me that he had reason to believe that Manny Wolf was a member of the Jewish Mafia and asked what I thought. (Manny was the Chairman of Allied Artists, which was Apollo's parent company which was in chapter 11 bankruptcy.)

Well, as to his first concern there was no denying that the company was flat broke; hedging this issue was not an option for me. Instead I pointed out that simply by virtue of entering into this agreement the company would be solvent. I also pointed out that our cash problem was the reason why I was not willing to negotiate either a lower rate than $28 per hour or waive the provision of being paid weekly, as we would need to make payroll for upwards of 200 employees. I told him that I knew the company would be profitable; but, the last thing that I wanted to see happen was not be able to perform on the contract due to cash flow problems. In this way, I learned to use Apollo's weakness as a negotiating tactic and it worked.

As to his second concern, I admitted that the company's business was slow but pointed out that this was actually a benefit to them because we had a number of qualified welders who could be recalled to work within a few days notice. He didn't ask and I didn't volunteer the actual number of welders who were on layoff, which was fortunate, because we only had about a dozen; but, I was sure that we would be able to hire 150 or more qualified welders in the Los Angeles area very quickly due to the high unemployment level in 1981. And I was correct. As a fall back position, if I had been asked about the number on layoff, then I would have told the truth by stating that I didn't know the exact number but that any shortfall could easily be made up by hiring welders from the greater Los Angeles metropolitan area due to the high level of unemployment.

As to the Jewish Mafia, I told him that since I had only known Manny for less than 3 months I could not vouch for him personally. I asked the reason for his concern and he said that he had heard that Manny was a member of La Costa. After informing him that La Costa was a luxury resort and spa we both had a good laugh. I sensed that he trusted me, or at least wanted to trust me, because he really needed to do this deal. To help further our relationship, I told John a short story of how Manny, along with his entourage of Jewish motion picture associates, would affectionately introduce me at meetings as their "token Gentile"! This not only got him laughing, but I believe that it put him at ease, as the "Jewish Mafia" became a non-issue.

MONEY AT 100% INTEREST RATE?

While I was finalizing the contract with Grumman, Manny filled me in on the financing agreement he had negotiated with B&B Sales, which was an Oklahoma based company that imported Romanian oil drilling well equipment for the U.S. market. He told me that he didn't respect them because they had all changed their Jewish names - Ron Howard, for example, was previously Ron Horowitz.

I flew to Oklahoma to see B&B's operation and to meet with Ron, as Manny wanted me to be their main contact for our borrowing. This was a $2,000,000 financing agreement that he had negotiated but it was the worst one-sided agreement that I had ever seen. With all due respect to Manny, he had exhausted all other possibilities and this was it. In 1980 the prime interest rate hit a record 21.5% and the money markets were really tight; so, we were over a barrel, and B&B knew it. After reading the agreement and subsequently discussing the mechanics of how the convoluted document worked, I told Manny it was ironic that the financing agreement that he had put together to save the company was actually going to be the final nail in our coffin! Per my analysis, I proved to him that the effective annual interest rate for borrowing their money was 100%! I was a little surprised when he said, "They just set the Jew business back by 100 years!" but then again, that was Manny, and you just had to love him, or so I thought at the time.

The convoluted formula for borrowing included an outrageous transaction fee for both borrowing and paying off the loan for each secured vehicle that was financed. Since each vehicle was financed for only an average of about 30 days until it was sold, the fees were eating us alive.

Manny had already borrowed $1,000,000 against the line of credit, so I insisted that he renegotiate the agreement as soon as possible. To my amazement, he said that since he had put the deal together, it would be <u>inappropriate for him to complain about the interest rate</u> and therefore it was now **my problem to handle!** Say what? Subsequently, one of his associates told me that Manny was convinced that our financiers were in the Jewish Mafia and he didn't want to piss them off. Was everyone paranoid or what? I guess the changing of their names was the least of his concerns. In any event, I started feeling a little less like a "token gentile" and a little more like a "sacrificial lamb"! I figured that as long as they got their money back with interest, then no heads would roll, and turned to the task of finding alternative financing to payoff B&B.

On the strength of the projected profits from the Grumman contract and my overall plans for Apollo, Manny introduced me to Peter Strauss at Peter's home in the Trousdale Estates of Beverly Hills in an effort to have me persuade him to lend us money (Peter was previously a top executive at Allied Artists and not the actor by the same name). Peter eventually agreed to fund the company up to $800,000 at the prime interest rate provided we were willing to personally invest the balance of $450,000. Manny put in $200,000, I put in $100,000 and several of Manny's personal friends invested the balance of $150,000.

One of the best days of my life was cutting a check to B&B Sales for $1,250,000, which represented $1,000,000 for the principal loan balance plus $250,000 in interest for 3 months at the effective 100% annual interest rate. We were all paid back with interest at the 21% prime rate within a year.

Subsequently, I heard that Peter reportedly was the largest investor in Barry Minko's Z-Best Carpet Cleaners, and we all know how that scam turned out. For those that don't know, the investors lost everything and Barry went to federal prison.

Had we not restructured Apollo's financing, we would not have been able to return the company to profitability and establish Apollo as the number one selling luxury motor home in 1981 according to the R.L. Polk retail registration report, which records the registration of all motor vehicles sold in the United States. Even though we had developed great products, it didn't hurt that Manny had excellent contacts in Hollywood. In fact, years before I joined the company, both Bob Hope and John Wayne had promoted its products in full-page print ads.

In retrospect, I learned that I should have obviously insisted on seeing the terms of the two million dollar line of credit that Manny had negotiated as a prerequisite to my joining the company. But then again, if I had not made the job change, then I would not have had this extraordinary experience, not to mention the opportunity to be Manny's "token gentile"!

I remember Manny referring to one of his past Allied Artist executives when he said, "I will never have that bastard ever work for me again for as long as I live; unless, of course, I need him." Yes, he was a real charmer.

"I like a man of his convictions, but don't quote me."
Anonymous

CHECKS AND TESTS

Never hire anyone without a general background check; and, if it is for a management position, then a credit check will be required as well. Credit problems are sometimes indicative of a larger underlying problem such as a drug or gambling addiction. These types of personal problems sometime lead an otherwise honest person to steal from their employer; and, if he or she is in a management position, then it is often way too easy for the company to be victimized in one way or another.

A pre-employment screening process should also include a physical exam and a drug test. The physical exam is necessary to help avoid future fraudulent worker's compensation claims involving prior injuries from being claimed to have happened after they were hired. A drug free work place should be part of the company's policy and a policy of random drug testing should also be included in the company's employee manual. Random tests should be administered on a regular basis, like once per month, and should include a minimum of 2% of the workforce. On the average, this will result in all employees being tested a minimum of once every four years. As a precondition of employment, any employee that fails a drug test will be fired without question.

To minimize the cost of pre-employment physicals and drug testing at one company we required new hires to pay the cost up front, which was reimburse only if they past the drug test. This never presented a problem as 100% of those tested passed the test and were reimbursed. The reason for the 100% success rate was that the ones who were dirty knew it and they didn't want to spend $50 of their money and end up not being hired, so they simply looked for other employment elsewhere. Prior to instituting this policy it was costing the company an average of $1,000 per month for applicants who ended up failing the drug test.

CHECKS AND BALANCES

A friend, whom I will call Bob, told me a fascinating story about a bookkeeper that had swindled him out of $30,000. This was in the 1980's and she was using a checkbook with NCR paper that would record an impression of every check written. Sounds like a safe system, even for a bookkeeper that also generated and signed the checks, right? Well, what she did was really creative. She would place a piece of cardboard between the check and the NCR copy so that no impression would be made. She would then make the checks payable to cash and cash them. She covered her tracks by placing a blank piece of paper on top of the NCR copy and then wrote that the check was made payable to one of the company's vendors. When the bank statement arrived the following month she would reconcile the bank account and it would always balance out. She certainly found her "little bit of genius"! This could have been a perfect crime; but, and this is the best part of his story, she got caught.

On the first of the month she had given her two weeks notice; and knowing that the bank statement would arrive within 10 days after the end of each month, she would then be able to reconcile the statement to correspond with the checkbook balance to cover her tracks before departing for Oregon. Well, to her surprise, upon receiving her resignation Bob told her that she could leave immediately and that he would pay her for two weeks without having to work. Her strong resistance to leaving right away gave him his first clue that something was not right; so, he insisted that she leave that day. A week later he received the bank statement and noticed a few of the checks were made out to cash but the checkbook imprint showed them as made payable to vendors! Her endorsement of the checks was the smoking gun. Through a mutual friend he learned which flight she was going to be on and hopped another flight that would arrive in Oregon an hour before she arrived. Bob confronted her at the airport terminal and presented her with the evidence while informing her of the prison time that she would be spending. She coughed up $25,000 in cash, which she was carrying in her purse while at the same time pleading for him not to seek prosecution and he agreed.

The lesson is to always have checks and balances to protect your company. Specifically, **never have the same person who signs the checks be responsible for the checking account reconciliation**.

Oh, and guess what, this story is far from over. Were you thinking that it was a mistake for Bob not to have had her arrested because she would most likely find another unsuspecting victim? Since I was thinking exactly the same thing, I asked him why he had been so forgiving or compassionate. Well, to my surprise, he started laughing uncontrollably and said that since his business partner didn't know about the embezzlement he simply pocketed the cash. He looked like the cat that ate the canary when he told me that it was $25,000 of tax-free money, as the IRS would never be the wiser. He was still grinning when he told me how she had unwittingly embezzled money for his benefit. In retrospect, I guess that this was the perfect crime after all. I learned that my friend had a dark side to him that I had not previously known. Remember integrity? Well, he lost his.

This story raises the opportunity for yet another lesson. From the perspective of a "silent partner" or as a private investor in a company that is being run by others, you will need to ensure that safeguards are in place to protect your interests. This is never easy and will definitely require some additional effort on your part.

As an example, when I became a 50% owner of MTC Corporation I insisted on performing the bookkeeping duties. I didn't want to risk offending my new partner by saying that I didn't know him well enough to trust him; so, I convinced him that not only would we be saving the cost of a bookkeeper, since I would perform these duties at night for free, but that it would give me invaluable insight into the business for cost consulting purposes. Yes, just another example of a win/win solution.

DON'T LET THE BASTARDS SUE YOU

Life is way too short to be spending your time in court, unless, of course, you are an attorney. Years ago I learned that a great alternative to financial disputes is to come up with a deal that they can't refuse. I once received an invoice that was in dispute and the other party was not willing to be flexible in the least, so it was basically pay the invoice or be sued. Well, in the spirit of a unilateral compromise, I mailed a check for 65% of the invoice and wrote on the backside of the check "Endorsement of this check acknowledges payment in full". I did not include a cover letter and simply waited for the check to clear the bank.

The reason why I didn't enclose a letter was two fold. Firstly, I didn't want to state my position in writing, since what you say can and will be used against you, and in the event it would go to trial I didn't want to risk making even the slightest misstatement of the facts. Secondly, and more importantly, I didn't feel that it would be helpful to rehash the issues and risk aggravating the situation any further.

In life there will inevitably be legitimate misunderstandings as well as people that try to take advantage of you. I have found that in both cases it is best to make a compromise despite the other side's stated objection to a settlement. I have not found it necessary to take this approach very often, but when I have it has worked 100% of the time. The primary reason for its success was because I would cough up a little more money than I thought that the service was actually worth as a compromise. I also knew that the other party would be hard pressed to not cash the check once it was in their hot little hands.

"A bird in the hand is worth two in the bush." Anonymous

MONEY DOESN'T BUY YOU HAPPINESS

While President of Executive Industries I had the pleasure of being invited to a dinner party at Ted Field's house in Beverly Hills. I was actually invited by the owner of one of our largest suppliers, Barry Bowman, who was Ted's then father-in-law, whose daughter, Susan was married to Ted. Well, Barry told me that Ted was the heir to the Marshall Field's department stores and had inherited $600,000,000 but had invested well and was worth a great deal more in 1988. His home was a 30,000 square foot Spanish style house on 3 acres (it was used in the Arnold Schwarzenegger film <u>Commando)</u>. Running their household was like operating a small business. Susan had a personal secretary, five nannies rotating 8-hour shifts 7 days a week, a nutritionist, a chef, two full time bodyguards, two maids and two full time gardeners. Couple this with a similar situation at their house in Santa Barbara and you become a slave to your possessions as Barry relayed to me several years later after Ted and Susan got divorced. As the saying goes, "money doesn't buy you happiness".

I have no idea if either Ted or Susan is happy today; but, what I have learned is that money absolutely doesn't buy you happiness; and, in fact, some of the richest people are the most miserable people in the world. It is difficult to believe, but if you really think about it, if you could have everything that you desire today, then what is there to look forward to in the future and what is there to motivate you? I know for a fact that if I had everything given to me, I would not have had the thrill of challenges, the passion for business and the satisfaction that comes with successful outcomes because I would not have had a financial incentive. There will always be some failures along the way and that is what we call "experience"; but the journey will always be a thrilling ride, so embrace it in whatever you do as that is life.

As a qualification, I would like to point out that up to a certain point money can buy you happiness in having the basic necessities of life and in having the peace of mind that comes with a feeling of financial security, however, beyond that point money will not make you any happier.

"Having more money doesn't make you happier. I have 50 million dollars but I'm just as happy as when I had 48 million." Arnold Schwarzenegger

HAPPINESS IS JUST A STATE OF MIND

Always keep a positive attitude because a negative one not only pays no dividends, but it also erodes employee's confidence in you. So how do you do this? I highly recommend reading <u>The Power of Positive Thinking</u> by Norman Vincent Peal. Positive thinking is the cornerstone of leadership. You must have a "can do attitude". The glass is **always** half full. You can either decide to be positive and focus on the upside or you can be negative and focus on the downside. Either way, the choice is 100% yours; just like in life, you can either be happy, or not, depending on your perspective. Don't make other people responsible for your happiness because then it is in their hands and not yours, where it should be. Don't be irresponsible with the responsibility for your happiness. After all, **"happiness is just a state of mind"**. <u>Yes, it really is as simple as that.</u> You and only you can create and control your thoughts or state of mind. In Plato's words, "The first and best victory is to conquer self. To be conquered by self is, of all things, the most shameful and vile." Successful people have control of their minds by being positive thinkers.

As an example, let's say that you are driving to work and get a flat tire, which makes you late for work. Well, you can choose to either let this experience completely ruin your day by being in a rotten mood, or you can choose to be happy because the flat tire did not cause an accident, or because your spare tire was not flat, or because it didn't happen on the freeway, or because it wasn't raining, or simply because you had been lucky not to have had a flat in more than 7 years.

Every situation in life is relative; things could always be worse so there really are a lot of things to be thankful for but you must actively think about them and not simply take them for granted, as most people do. The perfect example is the guy who was upset because he had no shoes until he saw a man who had no feet.

<u>If you always make your desires a preference and not an addiction, then you will not be setting yourself up for agonizing frustration and disappointment</u>. Addictions make you a slave. **Making your desires preferences may be the single most important aspect of living a happy life.** You must be willing to let go of something that you desire before you can be at peace.

Your success should be measured in terms of your happiness and not by your financial wealth. You will find happiness in doing and not just in possessing. If your wealth does not translate to happiness, then it is absolutely worthless; however, happiness can nonetheless be found in the process of accumulating wealth with all of its exciting challenges.

The primary motivator in my career was never big money, but rather the challenge and satisfaction of being able to do what I knew I was capable of doing by applying myself to the fullest. I always knew that the money would naturally follow, but I was never preoccupied with how soon I would acquire it. In retrospect, had I focused on a deadline for wealth, then I would have had a more difficult time getting past setbacks that I had to overcome during my career. It is good to have long-term goals, but **we all live in the present, so that is where we must find our happiness.** In other words, take one step at a time and enjoy the journey. As a great philosopher once said, "It is not the destination, but the journey that is most important." Our happiness should be found in the satisfaction that we find in our daily lives, which has its own immediate rewards. **Never postpone your happiness**.

There is a lot of truth in the following quote from Lao Tzu (A great Chinese philosopher):

"If you are depressed, you are living in the past.
If you are anxious, you are living in the future.
If you are at peace, you are living in the present."

In 1976 Ottie Alburn, the owner of Vogue Coach, sold a stock in which he made a $750,000 profit but he was beside himself because he had to pay $250,000 in taxes. He was so upset that he complained non-stop for a week. Well, right then and there I made a pledge to myself that if I were ever lucky enough to make that kind of money that I would not complain about paying my taxes. In fact, I told myself that I would love to make so much that I would have to pay $250,000 in taxes. Who wouldn't? Well, Ottie for one!

I eventually ended up making the "big bucks", and I am proud that not once have I ever begrudged paying my taxes and have simply been happy with the portion that I got to keep. After all, paying taxes is the cost of admission, or the cost of doing business. If I had not witnessed and learned a lesson from Ottie's misery years earlier, then I wouldn't have made that pledge to myself and most likely would not have been happy with the portion that I got to keep, just like Ottie.

"Success is getting what you want. Happiness is wanting what you get." Dale Carnegie

KNOW WHAT YOUR EMPLOYEES WANT

What is an employee's highest priority? How would you rank their priorities? I have found that how you rank your employee's priorities is the key to successfully manage and keep good employees. Would you say that an employee's top priority is pay? If you said yes, then you would be wrong. Would you say it is the people that they work with? Once again, you would be wrong. How about the type of work? Well, you are getting warmer, but still wrong. Don't even say vacation time or other benefits as they are not even in the top four.

An employee's top priority is job security. Yes, everyone would like more money, but nobody wants to worry about not having a job. I know that this may seem obvious but it is surprising to me how few managers actually capitalize on this knowledge of their employee's basic and top priority. Moreover, there are two additional priorities ahead of pay level for most employees: the type of work they perform and the people with whom they work.

Job security is an employee's <u>top priority</u>; however, depending on the economy and more specifically how it affects his or her place of employment, job security may or may not be their <u>top concern</u>.

It is usually only during tough times that an employee's top priority of job security becomes his or her top concern. In other words, employees are not always preoccupied with losing their job, but job security is nonetheless their top priority. Only those who are either overconfident or foolhardy will throw caution to the wind at their own peril. This is the reason why most employees will either not ask for a raise or will not be too aggressive in asking for one.

So, how do you give your employees job security? Well, favorable comments and giving deserved credit are a great start. In fact, this has often been considered more valuable to an employee than a raise because favorable feedback reinforces one's self-esteem and value to the company, which creates a greater sense of job security. It should go without saying that an employee who does not have job security will be looking for a new job. An employee's job security will help reduce employee turnover. Complimenting job performance also improves employee morale and better job performance. I have been amazed at how few managers praise their employees.

Once I asked a manager why he would always criticize his employees when needed but never praised them. His shocking response was that he was afraid to praise them for fear of having them ask for a raise and it was his job to keep the costs down!

During a severe economic downturn, I needed to reduce production by 20%. I could have simply informed our employees via a memo that business was lousy and we needed to layoff 20% of our employees. Unfortunately, with a 10% unemployment rate at the time, I knew that any laid off employees would have a difficult time finding other employment. Consequently, I gathered all 500 employees and very passionately explained that I didn't want to lose a single employee, as we valued each and every one of them.

I told them that I would rather have some employees leave for other employment opportunities than to have to lay off someone who may not be able to find other employment. Therefore, in lieu of a 20% layoff, I announced that we would be cutting back their hours by 20% via a 4-day workweek. I was absolutely shocked by their standing ovation. Okay, to be honest, even though they were standing and applauding, we only had 10 chairs in the plant so everyone was already standing. Nonetheless, it was a great moment and technically speaking it actually was a standing ovation!

I made no promises of how long the reduced hours would last, but I told them that if enough employees voluntarily left for other jobs, this attrition would benefit the remaining employees by offering them increased hours. We ended up losing only a few employees and a number of employees were able to find part-time jobs on Fridays or Saturdays to make up for their reduction in pay. This approach not only increased morale due to eliminating an anticipated layoff during very uncertain times, but it also brought us closer together. I also made it clear that all of the office staff and management were on a reduced pay program and that no one was going to have their pay reinstated unless everyone was reinstated, as we were all in this together for better or for worse. Having had to layoff a number of employees during my career, I found that this approach gave me a great sense of comfort. Keep in mind that firing someone for cause is always difficult; however, it is infinitely more difficult to layoff good employees through no fault of their own.

During that meeting I shared the company's business plan and status, which subsequently lead to our employees asking me to give them monthly updates and I agreed. These updates were a great stepping-stone for not only helping to alleviate their anxiety but also to form an even closer bond; one built on trust and honesty. It also gave me a great opportunity to let them know what they could do to help; I emphasized improving product quality and cost saving efficiencies.

<u>Loyalty is a two-way street. You cannot expect employees to be loyal to the company if it is not loyal to them in return.</u>

Treating your employees as you would like to be treated is a great policy.
Job security will always be an employee's top priority, even if they don't talk about it; so, never take it for granted.

"A compliment does no good, unless the person being complimented hears it." Anonymous

THE POWER OF "THANK YOU"

Never assume that others know that you appreciate them. These two words "thank you" cost you absolutely nothing. It is so easy to say; yet far too few people ever say it or at least not often enough. I have learned that a simple "thank you" will make people want to continue to help you. It is not just a polite thing to say; it is also a sincere acknowledgment to someone for something that they did, regardless of how small.

Early in my career and shortly after becoming a newly minted vice president of a company I received a Christmas card from the president of the company with a hand written note attached which read, "Mike, I want to thank you for everything that you do for the company. It has been a great year and I just want you to know how much I appreciate your dedication and hard work, and how much I look forward to working with you next year."

I had been staying with my folks at the time (great food), as I had returned to California from Arkansas earlier that year to take this new job; so, the Christmas card had been sent to their address and I naturally was proud to share it with them. After reading his note, I believe that my mother was more proud of me than she had been at my graduation. That was 40 years ago and I will never forget the power of that "thank you"; it really made me feel great, as I am sure it would make anyone.

Over the course of my career I followed his example and sent a number of "thank you" cards of my own and I only hope that they were received with as much appreciation and pride as mine.

It is my belief that these cards, in deed, played an important part in coalescing a loyal management following over the course of 40 years.

Interestingly enough, eight years later I filled the shoes of that president whom I had always admired and respected.

NEVER LET YOUR ATTORNEY MAKE BUSINESS DECISIONS FOR YOU

I have learned, without exception, that attorneys will always err on the side of being conservative; they have absolutely nothing to gain and everything to lose by being a risk taker. It is like giving a friend advice about investing their hard earned money. You would never want them to make risky investments on your advice and then see them lose their money. Being in business is always a risk by definition. Being an informed risk taker is what business is all about. That is **your job. It cannot be delegated.**

By the same token, never make a business decision involving legal issues that you do not clearly understand without first consulting your attorney because legal issues frequently present significant risks that you need to recognize and take into account.

LEGAL DOCUMENTATION

Whenever there is a possibility that your company may have an exposure to a lawsuit get in the habit of organizing files with chronological **self-notes** with backup data to support the company's position. Once a lawsuit is served, you may not have the time to pull all the information together, nor will you remember all of the little details that may make the difference in the case. This is the same type of mindset that hopefully you develop in school by preparing for your final exams and organizing your work-studies on a daily basis with important self-notes as opposed to developing the bad habit of cramming for an exam the night before. By being super organized, you will also find that you will have less time-related stress.

GIVING A DEPOSITION

While I am not an attorney and am not giving legal advice my experience has given me certain beliefs.

In a deposition, always answer the question that is asked and absolutely no more. Virtually everyone, other than a seasoned veteran, will make the mistake of saying too much in a deposition, as it is natural to speak your mind especially when you feel that you have nothing to hide and want to appear cooperative. Also, some peoples' egos compel them to educate the questioner by saying too much. In fact, most attorneys are a lot smarter than they let on to be in an attempt to trap the person being deposed. As an example, if you were asked if you have children, the correct answer would be either yes or no. The incorrect answer, which most people will give, is that they have three children, or that they have three children Mary, Tom and John, and they are 3, 5 and 7 years old respectively. Depositions are not unlike a job interview whereby a prospective employee will tell you a lot more than you could ever ask provided you first make them feel at ease. This is just another example of "What you say can and will be used against you" and many a case has been won or lost based on what unintentionally comes out in a deposition.

"Better to remain silent and be thought a fool, than to speak and remove all doubt." Abraham Lincoln

A BAD DECISION IS BETTER THAN
NO DECISION AT ALL?

Sometimes making decisions is difficult but they need to be made. The best advice is to weigh all of the pertinent information and evaluate the upside and downside of each prospective decision. For example, a critical component part for a product that is being manufactured in your facility has a history of having unreliable availability, and there is only one supply source. It is your job to ensure that the plant does not shut down due to a parts shortage, so what do you do? First, you analyze your usage requirements for that single source component and determine both your inventory level and purchase lead-time. Next, you decide how much of a cushion you need, which is the hard part. If you stock too much, then you may not have enough space for storage, or you may need to borrow money with the associated interest expense. On the other hand, if you stock too little, then you risk running out and shutting down the production plant. Both situations are a problem. The worst scenario is the risk of shutting down the plant; so, it is better to have too much inventory and pay interest and have storage problems than to shut down the plant, which would require layoffs and an interruption of the supply of your products to your valued customers.

Once a decision is made, it must be monitored regularly, because many things may change over time and may need corrective decisions. I have found that a bad decision is better than no decision at all because bad decisions can always be corrected with another decision; not making a decision is simply not an option for a decision maker in a position of responsibility. I have actually worked with high-level managers who believed that if you never make a difficult decision then you would never be found wrong! Surprisingly, they would allow their unqualified subordinates to make the difficult decisions and if something goes wrong they simply blame them. This is what I call "leading from behind". It is good to be cautious about your decisions, but you must always accept the responsibility for being the decision maker, as important decisions can't be delegated. However, if you find it necessary to delegate some or most of your responsibility, don't make the mistake of looking the other way, as you are still ultimately responsible.

A well-balanced management style or mindset of a decision maker cannot be dependent solely on quantitative analysis, but rather on a tolerance for an imperfect world. We must embrace flexibility and acknowledge that management structures are never perfect. The best managers are those that balance their people skills with their analytical analysis. They must recognize that less than perfect decisions must be made, profits must be generated and things must be accomplished to keep the company moving forward. What sets general managers apart is their overall knowledge. A truly well rounded manager will have a working knowledge of all areas of business including human resources, sales, marketing, manufacturing, purchasing, engineering, accounting and legal matters.

Continually monitoring and evaluating your decisions in a timely manner will allow you to take necessary corrective action before you are too far off the correct path. Despite how good you may think your past decisions may have been, never assume that they can't be improved upon.

This brings to mind a story of these two hunters who had downed an eight point deer in the thick underbrush several miles from their truck. To haul it back to their truck they decided to each grab its tail and pull it through the brush. They soon discovered that the tail was way too short for both of them to hold onto; they were tripping over each other; and the eight point antlers kept hanging up on the brush. It proved to be extremely slow going. After some discussion, one of the guys decided that it would be better to approach the deer from the other end and each grab one side of the antlers and back through the brush in order to keep the antlers from getting hung up. Not only were they able to each get a great grip and were no longer tripping over each other but the antlers were no longer getting hung up, hence the perfect solution. Well, after about 30 minutes, the one guy says to the other, "I really made a great decision, as we are going at least five times faster than before," but the other guy noted, "Yes, but we are getting farther and farther away from the truck!"

"I used to be indecisive, but now I'm not so sure." Tommy Cooper

READY, FIRE, AIM

Most decision-making is an intuitive process rather than an analytical one. This is referred to as "by the seat of your pants", or "gut feeling". If you are too analytical, the opportunity may pass you by while you are waiting for more data. "He who hesitates is lost"; and, as we all know, if you are a decision maker you can always correct a bad decision by making another decision.

"To be sure of hitting the target, shoot first and call whatever you hit the target." Ashleigh Brilliant

GIVING A SPEECH

The biggest fear in giving a speech is the fear of making a mistake and looking like a fool, which can ruin an otherwise excellent speech. You should not worry about making a mistake because absolutely everyone does and as my father would say, " God made very few perfect people." It helps to remind yourself that you are not perfect and trust me when I say that no one in the audience thinks you are either. If you make a mistake, just acknowledge it by making fun of it and move on. This approach will actually gain you support from your audience because everyone is human and it is not bad to acknowledge that you too are a humble human.

Just before he retired from the Tonight Show, after 30 years of a nightly show, Johnny Carson said that he was extremely nervous every night going on stage to give his monolog until he got his first laugh. Certainly, if Carson was still nervous after 30 years on the job, then it must be normal for everyone to experience a similar fear. The best approach is to relax and concentrate on the message that you want to communicate. If you really want to communicate a message, then just do it and do it with passion.

You would think that a well educated professional, like a doctor, would have enough confidence to be able to give a speech without being too nervous, right? My mother was a receptionist and nurse's assistant in a doctor's office in Pasadena, California and also the President of the Medical Assistant's Association. As the President of the association it was her responsibility to introduce the guest speaker at the association's monthly dinner. There were usually about 100 people in attendance, which included about 30 doctors and 70 assistants. Well her guest speaker, a prominent physician from another city, showed up for the dinner but when it was time for her to introduce him he had disappeared. She thought that he must have fallen ill or had an emergency but the next day he called her to apologize and told her the truth of why he had left. To her surprise, he said that when he had agreed to speak it was his understanding that he would be speaking to about 30 doctors but when he saw 100 people in the audience he simply freaked out since he had never given a speech to that may people before in his life! I was about 15 when she told me this story and rather than viewing public speaking as something I alone feared, I started viewing it as simply human nature which was one more thing that helped me to overcome my own fears.

Until I became President of Apollo Motor Homes at age 34, the largest group to which I had given a speech was 50 people in one of my graduate school classes. You can only imagine how nervous I was to have to address an audience of 500 of Apollo's customers! To help overcome my fear, I recalled everything that I had learned up to that time, prepared what I wanted to communicate and just tried to relax. After introducing my staff, and myself, I presented a 15-minute prepared speech and opened it up for a Q & A session. To my pleasant surprise, the interaction with the audience actually made me feel as relaxed and as comfortable as if

I were speaking to a small group of people in my office! It turned out to be a great experience and by the time I left the stage an entire hour had transpired. In retrospect, they couldn't shut me up! I learned that the interaction with the audience was infinitely more comfortable than just having your audience sit and stare at you. It also created a more intimate relationship and enforced my desire to really want to communicate what I was saying. However, just like Johnny Carson, I never totally got over my initial fears even after that great day.

As brilliant an orator as many think President Obama may be he essentially reads 95% of all his speeches from a teleprompter. This gives the appearance that he is speaking to his audience spontaneously off the top of his head with perfect cadence and excellent eye contact. Without a teleprompter he is far from brilliant, as he often refers to his notes and is often searching for the correct words as he frequently pauses and appears lost. My point is not to diminish our President but rather to point out that none of us are inferior to those whom we may think as superior. Most of us will never become excellent public speakers, and we don't need to be, but to be successful in business you must overcome the fear that most of us have in speaking up. If you aren't able to voice your opinion then you will be relegated to being a follower, which is no way to become successful in business.

Unless you have the use of a teleprompter, my best advice is to give your speech from the heart with passion and not read, memorize or overly rehearse it. You should know your topic well enough that all you should need is a 3x5 index card with key words as a reminder of what you want to talk about and in what order. Unless you have an excellent memory, relying on your memory will more likely than not make you nervous enough to forget something and in your panic blow the entire speech (life's awkward moments).

As an example, if you like a certain sport and know a lot about it, then how easy is it to talk with your friends about it without even referring to any notes? If your sport of choice happens to be football, then I am sure that you would be able to spontaneously talk about strategies, rules, penalties, relative strengths and weaknesses, players, positions, coaches, teams, formations, ratings, statistics etc. This should be your objective with every speech regardless of the topic. Become an expert on the topic and have the confidence that goes with it. (Whoever said to visualize your audience naked should be shot)

"Many believe that the biggest fear in life is giving a speech and the second greatest fear is that of dying, so if you find yourself giving a eulogy at a funeral, then you would probably be better off being in the box!" Johnny Carson

STRESS IS A GOOD THING?

Starting a new job, or changing jobs is one of the most stressful events in our lives, second only to the loss of a loved one. Stress is really not a bad thing if we know how to handle it. In fact, a certain amount of stress in our life is a good thing. We are eventually going to encounter stressful events of great magnitude in our life anyway; knowing how to handle smaller doses of stress along the way will help us in being able to cope with these major events when they happen.

As complex as human beings are, and with no owner's manual, we need to sort things out as we go and try to gain valuable insight from those who have preceded us. In How to Stop Worrying and Start Living Dale Carnegie stated a great truth when he says that when something bad happens it is human nature to blow the situation way out of proportion. Things are usually never as bad as we first imagine. Carnegie's advice was to rationally visualize how bad a situation could possibly be and then be able to accept it. The worst-case scenario will probably never happen; however, if you prepare yourself for it and know that you can survive it, then you will realize a tremendous amount of comfort knowing that you can handle the worst-case scenario. Then it becomes your objective to simply improve your situation by whatever means possible. Okay, this may not be so simple but at least you will be in a calmer state of mind, which is always best for effective problem solving.

Though there was always a certain amount of daily stress in my life, I can honestly say that I never totally stressed out, nor did I burn out (when my wife was proof reading this she said that this statement was not true; yet, I correctly pointed out that regardless of my stress level I was neither hospitalized nor institutionalized, and she agreed, so I kept it).

"If you think things can't get worse it's probably only because you lack sufficient imagination." Anonymous

PASSION, LEADERSHIP AND SALESMANSHIP

Even though you may not be in sales, you must be a great salesperson to be successful in business. You may never sell a product in your life, but in the business world you will **always** be selling yourself and your ideas. You must possess the <u>**passionate power of persuasion and the ability to effectively communicate**</u>, which is the **definition of salesmanship**.

For starters, get the best education possible; it will help provide you with a solid foundation of knowledge evoking a genuine feeling of empowerment. "Knowledge is power" and that builds confidence.

Once you have the knowledge and confidence in yourself, then all you need is to be sincerely **passionate** about what you set out to accomplish. If you are not 100% committed to an idea and not genuinely passionate about it, then you will have a difficult time convincing others.

If you find that you are just not passionate about what you are doing, you are in the wrong job. Life is way too short to be stuck in a job that you can't be passionate about as no one can do his or her best without passion. I have seen far too many people in the workplace who are not passionate about what they are doing and they are considered marginal employees at best. By contrast, this creates a tremendous opportunity for the truly passionate employees to excel.

The successful leader must create and then **passionately** promote and protect the values of the organization from everything to how employees are treated to their love of the company's products or services. By the treatment of employees I mean **instilling pride** in their work and **loyalty** to the company through training and their relations with management to foster a unified team spirit. **Pride is the stepping-stone to passion** whereby **employees will absolutely demand quality**, which must be built-in to a product and can neither be added-on nor become the sole responsibility of the quality control department. Protecting the company's values also means keeping true to its relationship with its customers from its administration of customer service and warranty policies to maintaining a superior level of quality products or services.

The successful leader must **passionately** embrace and manage a wide range of responsibilities from being a visionary with exciting and **creative ideas** to the nurturing and implementation of these new ideas to become **product innovations**. This is truly a job for a general manager with a wide range of talents and experience from sales and manufacturing to engineering and cost accounting. Being persistent and **passionate** are vital cornerstones for the successful manager. An excellent leader is one who also has the ability to bring together a diverse group of people with different beliefs and **passionately** unites them to believe in a common goal for the benefit of all.

The successful leader must constantly develop plans of action, and then organize and execute on those plans. I say "constantly" because almost all plans will require some adjustments depending on the changing business climate and the plan's effectiveness based on continuous feedback. The only thing that is constant in business is change, so most plans will be optimal at best and only for a period of time. Success must be nurtured and failures must be recognized and acknowledged quickly, but never prematurely; there is never room for denial.

I have known a number of successful sales people and most had to learn their trade while a select few were <u>natural born salesmen</u>.

Bud Cooper worked for me in sales at four companies. He worked in vehicle sales his entire life in both the auto and recreational vehicle industries, and was an extremely loyal and hard working employee who was always there when I needed him. He was also a top-notch musician who played the trombone and was a real character to boot. He loved people and would often liven up everyone's life with his creative antics. As an example, during a trade show in Colorado he was one of a ten man sales team and challenged everyone to a prank. They each chipped in $11 for a total pot of $110. He then explained that the first salesman to get a customer down on all fours (knees and elbows) would win the $100 pot with $10 going to the customer for being an unwitting participant. Bud ended up winning this challenge by convincing an unsuspecting customer that the company's vehicles were equipped with something that he just had to see to believe. This approach required him to feign excitement and to take the lead by going under the vehicle in hopes that his customer would be curious enough to follow him.

Bud loved ice cream and would always have several gallons in his office refrigerator at the dealership. Well, late one hot Saturday afternoon a family of four came into the dealership looking to buy a car. He had them almost 100% sold but he couldn't quite close the deal even with his standard offer of a $100 cash bonus for closing the deal by the end of that day. They told him that they were sold on the car but wanted to visit one more dealerships down the street before they closed and would call him by the end of the day with their decision. Bud responded by saying "Congratulations, I just realized that you are my 100th customer this month and as a consequence I have a gift for you." With that he went to his office and returned with a gallon of ice cream. Now, think about it for a minute, where are they going to go with a gallon of ice cream on a hot afternoon? You got it, straight home! An hour later they called him to finalize the deal and to secure the $100 cash incentive.

Bud was excellent at bonding with customers and coming up with new product ideas to satisfy their needs. He was an excellent listener. He knew the customer's needs better than any salesman whom I have ever known; he was **passionate** about the products that he sold and he was, in fact, a natural born salesman.

"I honestly think that it is better to be a failure at something you love than to be a success at something you hate." George Burns

ALWAYS QUESTION AUTHORITY AND "EXPERTS"

Never believe everything that is presented to you by an "expert". Always question those in authority because there are a surprising number of companies that have cooked their books in the past at a tremendous cost to their shareholders and creditors. A few examples are Enron, Global Crossing, Bernie Madoff's hedge fund, Ascot Partners, and Jon Corzine's MF Global.

Likewise, never believe everything that your stockbroker tells you, as there is a built-in conflict of interest since your broker only is paid a commission when you either buy or sell a stock. Most stock offerings have a lot of fine print in their Prospectus, so never invest until you read it completely. I have read several offerings that had a Prospectus that was about 50 pages long and buried in those pages were disclaimers, which in not so many words essentially said that the risks are so great that you would have to be a fool to invest in their company. Well, your broker will probably tell you that it is really a good stock and that the language in the Prospectus is just "standard protective language" and not to worry about it. All I have to say is that if the company goes south with your hard earned money, then the officers of the company are off scot-free because all of the investors were properly warned in advance in writing. As the old saying goes, "Let the buyer beware."

STATISTICS ARE MORE THAN JUST NUMBERS

"Figures don't lie, but liars figure." Samuel Clemens

Never take statistics at face value, as more often than not there are more to numbers than meet the eye. For example, would you book a flight with an airline that boasts of only having three crashes out of ten million flights over the past 50 years? Sounds pretty safe, right? Well, what if I told you that two of the three crashes happened just last week! Are you having a change of mind?

As a CFO (Chief Financial Officer) of public companies, I always enjoyed the challenge of preparing annual financial reports because it included a narrative of the company's performance as a percentage comparison to the prior year. A 900% increase in profits as compared to the prior year certainly sounds fantastic; however, when viewed with an eye on the actual magnitude of the profit, a 900% increase could simply mean that the profits increased from $10 to $100! Not so fantastic after all.

As a cautionary note, don't get confused with percentage increases. For example, if you quadruple a number, then you have actually increased it by 300% and not 400%. Most people get confused; so let me give you some examples. When a number is doubled it is a 100% increase. Using 10 as a starting base number, every time the base number increases by itself, or by 10 in this example, it is a 100% increase. Therefore, an increase from 10 to 30 would be 200% and an increase from 10 to 40 would be 300%.

I have also seen even more confusion when it comes to discounts. If a product's price increases by 50%, then what discount would be required to get the price back down to the original price before the price increase? A 50% increase would require a 33-1/3% discount to return it to its original price (i.e. 10 to 15 is a 50% increase and 15 to 10 is a 33-1/3% reduction).

You must be able to think clearly and keep your wits about you when evaluating what you are being told. As an example, if Mary's mother had four daughters and three of the daughters were named April, May and June, then what was the fourth daughter's name? Don't feel badly if you said "July", but if you said "Mary", then you would be correct (clue: <u>Mary's mother</u>).

"A statistician is someone who is good with numbers, but lacks the personality to be an accountant." Anonymous

"82.7% of all statistics are made up on the spot." Steven Wright

PAY RAISES

Always remember that a pay raise is only justified on the basis of job performance and a person's value to the company. **Raises are never justified based on an employee's need for more money**. If people need more money, then they must either work harder or smarter in order to justify being worth more to the company. An employee's inability to manage his or her money, or live within their income, is not the company's problem as long as they are being paid a fair or competitive wage.

On numerous occasions I have had employees try to justify a raise solely because they wanted to buy a luxury car or a more expensive house. Don't be that guy. On one occasion I actually had a well-paid executive inform me that his tax accountant told him that he needed to make more money! He was a smart guy; so, I expected that he must have thought about what he was going to say to me, but this was the best he could come up with? Give me a break! Okay I will say it again, don't be this guy either.

Never ask for a raise too aggressively unless you have lined up another job; your boss may feel that it is not justified and your attitude toward the denial may signal to him or her that you are a disgruntled employee and proceed to find your replacement.

Don't be in a rush for a pay raise or promotion; your mindset should be one of patience. In the early years of your career the learning process should be so great that you should actually be paying your employer for the experience. After all, how many applicants didn't get hired? Take comfort in the fact that all good managers will want to keep and promote the best and the brightest (you).

We once had an employee working on our motor home assembly line who installed the carpeting so fast and efficiently that we decided to make an example of him for others to emulate. This was in 1975 and he was making $5 per hour which was the average shop rate at the time; however, after a series of merit increases, his pay doubled within 6 months. He literally was doing the work of two and he just loved working fast. Usually pay is very confidential; but, we made it known that he was getting pay increases without divulging his actual pay rate; we left it up to him to leak it if he wanted which we hoped he would. <u>Rewarding good behavior is one of the best things you can do to promote an employee's sense of pride and loyalty to the company</u>.

Your objective should always be to set yourself apart from others by learning as much as possible and by applying yourself to the fullest. Opportunities will come in one form or another and it will be your good judgment that dictates your path to success. You must be prepared to grab the brass ring. When you are ready it should be self-evident; however, if you have self-doubts and hesitate, then that opportunity may forever pass you by. In my case, I never wanted to look back on my life and have any regrets, so I constantly pushed myself despite inherent risks.

KNOW YOUR LIMITATIONS

Never commit to anything that is either beyond your area of expertise or not within your time frame of acceptability as you will always want to <u>give more than you promise</u> and in a timely manner. Therefore, never be afraid to admit that you are not totally qualified to handle a project, as your boss may not know your limitations as well as you do.

"Fools rush in where wise men fear to tread." Alexander Pope

PATENTS, TRADEMARKS AND TRADE DRESS

While I am not an attorney and am not giving legal advice my experience has given me certain beliefs.

As a good friend often said, "The first guy never has a chance". Unless you can secure a patent on an idea, it will be easy for those who follow to not only copy but to improve upon your idea. It is immensely easier to improve on someone's idea than to create a new one from scratch; so, you will obviously want to protect your idea with a patent. In weighing the cost of the patent versus its value to you, always be aware that making small design changes can sometimes easily circumvent patents. Also, the cost of defending a patent in court may be too high to pursue. However, if you do not defend your patent, trade dress or mark, after it has been used by someone in commerce you risk losing your rights, as it will be considered to be a part of the public domain; you must plan accordingly. Patents have a term of 20 years, at which time they will be considered a part of the public domain. Design patents, unlike utility patents, have a term of 14 years from the date of issue. Trademarks on the other hand can last forever provided that they are renewed at 5, 10 and 20 years following the date of registration, and every 10 years thereafter. Your trade dress protection has no expiration date and there are no filing requirements. If you are ever challenged on your trade dress rights, then the burden will be on you to prove that you were the first to the market place with your product's unique features. Meeting this requirement can be as simple as providing copies of your original advertisements and the dates the ads ran in a newspaper or trade magazine.

If you are unfamiliar with the term "Trade Dress", it is basically the appearance of a product or its packaging. A violation of someone's trade dress may result in a lawsuit whereby there is an allegation that someone copied a competitor's product or packaging of its product for the purpose of piggybacking on the marketing and advertising of an established product in the market place. In order to prevail in a trade dress lawsuit you must prove that your competitor caused <u>confusion in the market place</u> due to a similar appearance to your product or packaging. In other words, you would be required to prove that a <u>customer may be confused enough by the similarities to actually purchase your competitor's product while thinking they were buying your product</u>.

It is best to consult with a professional regarding this subject matter, as it can be very complex and the laws may change over time.

TO BE SUCCESSFUL, ALWAYS PLAN AHE
A
D

No one has a crystal ball but give the people who work for you the benefit of your best estimate of your view of the company's future, and update them over time as things change or as you get closer in time to locking in your plans. This is especially helpful in a manufacturing business; it gives the purchasing department the opportunity to plan for a possible increase in material requirements on long lead-time items. It also allows for pre-planning for the acquisition of both the required production personnel and tooling requirements to support production. Once the decision is made to put a plan into action it will be too late for the purchasing department to advise you that it can't support the plan due to projected parts shortages. It always pays to be prepared for possible contingency plans well in advance.

The first that I learned about planning ahead was from a classmate in 5th grade when I was 10. His name was Steve MacPherson, an extremely friendly and gregarious classmate who has remained a lifelong friend.

Since neither of us knew when to stop talking in class we spent a certain amount of time together every week in detention after school. The penalty was always the same: report to the detention room at 3 pm and don't leave until you have written 500 times "I will not talk in class" (very creative). It would usually take about an hour and was 5 pages long with 100 times per page.

Well, one day after just 20 minutes in detention Steve walked to the front of the class and turned in his 5 pages. Wow, 20 minutes! Pep Baldwin had held the prior record of 30 minutes by mastering the art of writing two lines simultaneously, which was facilitated by the joining of two pens together using rubber bands (patent pending). Pep eventually went on to become the president of his family's business.

The detention room monitor was a little surprised at Steve's speed, so he instructed him to write an additional page of 100 times before he would release him. With that Steve went back to his desk and within 5 minutes he returned with another full page of original inked "I will not talk in class"! So what was Steve's secret (no copies, all inked originals)?

Since I was still in detention for another half hour that day, I could hardly wait to see Steve the next day to ask him his secret and he said, "Since I know that I will be in detention for talking in class at least once per week, I prepare my sheets every night and during the weekends while watching television." He then showed me his clipboard, which contained enough sheets to last him through the balance of the school year! Not surprisingly, Steve eventually went on to become the president of his family's business as well.

"Plan your work and work your plan." Vince Lombardi

NEVER CALL YOUR CUSTOMERS PRICKS

The devil is in the details. Never overlook the importance of personally reviewing all written documents and letters; just one small error could cost you big time. About 40 years ago, when I was starting my career as vice president of a manufacturing company, I had the responsibility of communicating with customers in an attempt to improve customer relations and avoid lawsuits. I dictated a letter to be sent to a disgruntled customer by the name of Mr. Price, and in my rush, I signed the letter without proof reading it first. Unfortunately, my secretary had typed a "k" instead of an "e"; so, the letter started out "Dear Mr. Prick . . . ". Oh what a difference a single character can make in the meaning of a word! What are the odds that a simple typo would actually spell a word? Needless to say, my letter didn't help resolve Mr. Price's problem, but I did learn an important lesson the hard way which has served me well for the past 40 years.

Fortunately, when I spoke to Mr. Price on the phone a week later he had a great sense of humor and we were able to make good headway in ultimately resolving his problem.

Mark Twain once said, "The difference between the almost right word and the right word is really a large matter – it's the difference between the lightening bug and the lightening."

THE TRUE CHARACTER OF A PERSON

My sister-in-law, Karen Fonger, taught me a lesson of how her boss identified potential managerial talent within the organization. He would arrive early at work before his employees and distribute trash between the building and the parking lot. Most employees simply stepped over or walked past the trash; however, on occasion someone, inevitably a future manager, would pick it up and place it in the trashcan.

You never know who may be watching so it will serve you well by getting into the habit of doing the right thing as both a good citizen and a good employee.

"True character is measured by what we do when we think no one is looking." H. Jackson Brown, Jr.

DON'T TAKE A PERCENTAGE OF THE PROFITS

I learned the hard way that it is best not to take a percentage of the profits as a form of your compensation. It is way too easy for the profits to be diluted by inflating the expenses or other creative accounting techniques.

I had joined a privately owned company just after its first quarter in which I was told the company had made a profit of $500,000. Being in charge of manufacturing, it was my responsibility to increase production as fast as possible in order to keep up with the ever-increasing sales demand. My efforts would be rewarded with 3% of the annual profit in excess of the $500,000 of profit already booked in the first quarter.

During the balance of my first year we substantially increased production and sales. Since the fixed overhead remained a constant, I figured that the company probably made a profit of at least $2,000,000 after the first quarter and I was really looking forward to a nice $60,000 payday. A large bonus was almost a no-brainer because even without any increase in sales we would still have at least replicated the first quarter for a three quarter profit of $1,500,000. Therefore, at a bare minimum it was like a guarantee of a $45,000 bonus, which was a lot of money in the 1970's.

Well, after the accountants got finished the company had only made a $500,000 profit, and that was for the entire year! The only way that this could be possible was if the company was actually losing money prior to my arrival.

I couldn't say for sure that they were being dishonest, so I gave them the benefit of the doubt and assumed that they were just stupid (I guess I was as well).

Since I had proven my worth, I received a large raise and my bonus plan was changed to a more verifiable metric that was based on production and sales numbers. I stayed with the company for five additional lucrative years and simply looked at my first year as an initiation fee.

In retrospect, since the company was privately owned, the owner would have had to pay $1,000,000 in state and federal taxes had the company made a $2,500,000 profit for the year (no doubt there was some creative accounting going on).

By the same token, never contribute to a charity or non-profit without first finding out what percentage of your contribution actually goes to the cause. The biggest scam is to tell you that 100% of the profits go to the cause; what they don't tell you is that after they take their fat salaries and deduct their lavish expenses, the profits are only 5% of the contributions. This means that only 5% of your contribution actually is going to the cause! And the saddest thing of all is that it is legal. There will always be salaries and expenses in any organization, but I personally will not contribute to any organization where less than 80% goes to the cause.

Your performance bonus should always be tied to an easily verifiable metric, like attaining a certain production or sales level.

NEVER SET YOUR OWN HOURS

Unless it is your own business or you are the president of a company, don't make the mistake of setting your own hours as both your peers and subordinates may view this as the height of arrogance. Business is a team sport and you are never so important that you do not have to conform to the company's business hours. It is a form of disrespect to the other employees (peers and subordinates), who count on being able to interface with you during regular business hours in order to perform their work.

KNOW-IT-ALL'S

"People who think they know everything are a great annoyance to those of us who do!" Isaac Asimov

Seriously, be confident in what you know, but not at the expense of others. Making others feel stupid will never accrue to your benefit, so don't.

"If I agreed with you, we'd both be wrong." Anonymous

DON'T PUT ALL YOUR EGGS IN ONE BASKET

The Art of the Deal is the title of Donald Trump's book. His basic message, which makes a lot of sense, is to take as little risk as possible and be willing to give up a larger ownership of the deal in order to reduce your personal risk. This allows you to not only protect your downside in each deal but it also allows you to participate in more deals to diversify your holdings. Not having all of your eggs in one basket is always good advice.

WHAT IS EXPERIENCE?

It has been said, "Experience is what you get when you don't get what you wanted". Good and bad experiences are nonetheless good learning experiences, which is what life is all about. Over time, it is these experiences that make us who we are; and, by learning from our past experiences we become better decision makers and avoid past mistakes.

Your choices will have resulting consequences, whether good or bad, but the bottom line is that the choice is yours.

"Experience is something you don't get until just after you need it." Steven Wright

"Experience is that marvelous thing that enables you to recognize a mistake when you make it again." Anonymous

"Good judgment comes from experience, and experience...........well, that comes from poor judgment." Anonymous

ACCOUNTING

It is absolutely critical for a future in business to clearly understand accounting. Understanding the financial numbers in your business is like understanding the heartbeat of your company, which may flat-line very quickly from a lack of sufficient cash even if it is profitable.

First, you need to have a general understanding of a financial statement. A **Financial Statement** is comprised of two basic elements, a **Balance Sheet** and an **Income Statement**.

The **Balance Sheet** is made up of only three basic elements: **Assets, Liabilities and Owner's Equity**. The understanding of the relationship between these three elements is one of the basics of accounting. The relationship is that the value of the Assets is always equal to the sum of the Liabilities plus the Owner's Equity. This relationship is represented by the formula: **Assets = Liabilities + Owner's Equity.** Make sure to commit this formula to memory, as it is the cornerstone of the Balance Sheet. As you already know from your algebra class, this formula can be written as: **Assets – Liabilities = Owner's Equity**. This allows you to visualize that the Owner's Equity is simply your Assets less your Liabilities. This should be easier to understand in this format, since your personal net worth, or owner's equity, is the total of all of your assets, or everything that you own, less the money that you owe to others. As a simplified example, if you own a $20,000 car and have $5,000 in your savings account, then your assets total $25,000. If you owe the bank $10,000 for the purchase of your car and have a student loan of $8,000, then your total liabilities are $18,000. Hence, your net worth or owner's equity is the difference of $7,000.

The **Income Statement** is simply a profit or loss statement for a specified period of time, like a month, a quarter or a year. The basic formula is simply represented by the formula: **Income = Net Sales - Expenses**

Performing bookkeeping and accounting functions is a great way to gain experience for becoming a manager or top executive of a company. If you dislike performing accounting functions, then keep in mind that it is just a stepping-stone to your future in becoming an astute businessperson, which can be an extremely rewarding career.

There is no better foundation for understanding and operating a business than a solid understanding of accounting. Being able to prepare financial statements will be invaluable to you in being able to analyze them. Analyzing financial statements will be a big part of your life and the better you understand accounting the better you will be in making decisions that affect the company's bottom line.

Being a Chief Financial Officer (CFO) can be a possible pathway to becoming the president of a company, since there would be no one in the company with a better understanding of its cost structure than you, an empowering position to say the least. Having said that, most companies promote sales and marketing people into the top position for two reasons; they not only know its customers and sales inside & out, which is the driving force of any company, but they also have the right personality to appeal to a larger segment of people both inside and outside of the company. Unfortunately, most accountants lack this type of personality, so if you are an accountant that also aspires to become a president of a company, then you will be best served by having a broader understanding of all aspects of a business. On the other hand, since most company presidents have worked their way up from the sales and marketing side of the business, they will definitely be reliant on the analysis and good judgment of their CFO, which can be a rewarding career as well.

DEPRECIATION EXPENSE

I had learned in business school that depreciation expense was a unique expense as it was not a cash flow item. I also learned that a capital expenditure was a cash flow item, but only a portion of it was an expense item on a scheduled depreciation basis. It was not until after I had graduated that I learned how some companies either didn't understand depreciation expense, or were being deceitful.

In the mid 1970's I was involved in an analysis of a golf course in Palm Springs as a potential investment, which looked promising, but had a small profit margin. Unfortunately, upon further analysis I realized that the depreciation expense was totally missing on their financial statements, which when added back made it a losing proposition. Also, on numerous occasions I have seen the depreciation expense represented in the cash flow statement. It is my belief that the former was deception and the latter was simply an accounting error, since there would be absolutely no benefit to the company to overstate their cash outflow. In any event, I learned to keep an eye on not only the existence of a depreciation expense, but also the assumptions of the useful life of the assets.

In order to project a more favorable financial forecast, I once saw a livery operator depreciate his vehicles up to 400,000 miles as its useful life. Even if you could stretch the useful mileage to

400,000 miles, the vehicle maintenance cost would be through the roof, not to mention the down time for repairs and the associated inconvenience to customers.

One of the most important things to consider when analyzing depreciation expense is the effect on cash flow when the equipment needs to be replaced. This capital expense can prove to be untenable for a company with either poor cash reserves or a lack of borrowing power. If the money is to be borrowed, then the additional cost of interest expense must also be included in your analysis.

Keep in mind that depreciation expense for tax purposes can be totally different from the actual business expense. Depending on the tax codes, some assets can be written off 100% in the year of acquisition, or on an accelerated basis. Financial statements should simply deal with the reality of the useful life of the asset and schedule the depreciation expense accordingly.

Once I was involved in an acquisition of a company that, due to the depreciated value of its assets, was actually worth a great deal more than its book value. This is frequently the case for companies that own developed real estate, which actually appreciates in value more often than not. This may also be true for other assets so you need to know what assets are on the company's balance sheet and not just the stated book value.

FINANCE

Other than my knowledge of Accounting and Algebra, the most valuable tool for decision-making was my knowledge of Finance. It allowed me to intelligently evaluate the most economical alternative between possible acquisitions. It also allowed me to choose the best offer from alternative offers.

The application of finance can be extremely complex; however, for the purpose of giving you an exposure to this field, I will offer you a simple example.

Would it be a better decision to purchase a machine today for $100,000 that will have a useful life of 30 years, or purchase a machine today for $60,000 that has a useful life of 15 years, and then purchase a replacement machine in 15 years for $70,000 that has a 15 year useful life (a total of $130,000)? Both alternatives give us a total useful life of 30 years.

In order to make an intelligent decision, you need two things; namely, the cost of funds and a Present Worth (PW) compound interest table. In this example we will assume that the cost of funds is 6% compounded annually. The cost of funds means the cost of borrowed money and PW tables are easily accessible.

The only way to compare these two alternatives is to determine the Present Worth (PW) for each alternative. By PW I mean the value or worth of each alternative today, or at the present time. Only in this way can their costs be compared head on. Otherwise, it would be like comparing apples to oranges.

Obviously the **PW of the first alternative is $100,000**, as it is what we would be required to pay today. The determination of the PW for the second alternative is a little more difficult. The PW is $60,000 plus the PW of spending $70,000 in 15 years from now. The calculations would be as follows:

PW = $70,000 x (the PW factor at 6% for 15 years). From the PW tables we know that the PW factor at 6% for a lump sum expenditure in 15 years is 0.4173; therefore, the PW = $29,211. This gives us a total **PW of $89,211** for the second alternative.

Consequently, the second alternative would be the best choice with a savings of $10,789, which is the difference between the two alternatives.

This was a simplified example; as it usually would be more complex with machine down time costs for maintenance, overhaul costs at periodic points in time and the respective scrap values at the end of the machines' useful life. Each of which would be required to be brought back in time to their present worth dollar amounts for comparison purposes.

As you can see, without a mathematical financial analysis you would be relegated to venturing a guess, which is no way to run the finances of a business or your personal life for that matter.

CHAPTER 4

AVOIDING ROADBLOCKS TO SUCCESS

Michael Hill

DON'T CHANGE JOBS TOO OFTEN

I have always subscribed to the idea of staying with a company for a minimum of 5 years since it never looks good on a resume to see a new employer every two to three years. If you do decide to leave after just a few years, then make sure you have a compelling reason to explain to a future employer; but, never badmouth your prior employer as bad mouthing never sounds good in an interview. Your prospective employer will always wonder if the reason was your fault or your employer's; you will need to have some credible specifics.

While I benefited by a number of job changes, my average tenure was still about six years, so I kept true to my own belief. My shortest tenure was just two years with Apollo; yet it was one of my greatest challenges and accomplishments up to that time, and yes, I had a very compelling reason, which I will explain a little later.

CLIMBING THE CORPORATE LADDER

Some employees have been promoted and have moved up the corporate ladder quickly by being very skilled at playing the dangerous game of politics. This approach can be extremely risky as it more often than not involves alienating or backstabbing others. The knowledge that someone is playing politics will expose him or her to being viewed as neither a team player nor a person of character.

Employees will be better served by promoting their own abilities and by developing a reputation of being someone who not only gets along with others but who is also supportive of others. The promotion of a rotten egg will not only reflect badly on whomever makes that poor decision but it will also make it difficult for the person being promoted to garner the support of his or her prior peers; a real recipe for failure.

I have never been tempted to play politics because it was not only inconsistent with my values but because I realized that it would be far easier and safer to simply prove my worth. I have always held a tremendous amount of respect and admiration for those in higher positions of authority. I have also held to a strong belief that my superiors would be smart enough to weed out the performers from the non-performers and promote the most deserving employees. I was never in a rush or impatient regarding pay raises or promotions; however, if I ever found that my beliefs were not well founded or that opportunities were limited, then and only then would I look for other employment opportunities.

Taking short cuts by playing politics can too easily backfire and result in your termination which would be a giant step backwards; so, don't.

"COME ON IN, THE WATER IS FINE!" Anonymous

After 6 years as Vice President of Operations for a recreational vehicle manufacturer, I jumped at the opportunity to become the President of Apollo Motor Homes. Apollo was a failing RV company, a wholly owned subsidiary of Allied Artists, a major motion picture company, which itself was in Chapter 11 bankruptcy at the time. As a turnaround company this was a formidable challenge to say the least. Five months before I was hired all five top executives resigned and walked off the job on the same day. It was my understanding that their action was due to a lack of cash, mounting losses, the complete shut down of the parent company, Allied Artists, and no banking relationship.

Manny Wolf, the Chairman of the Board for Allied Artists, recruited me for the job. I really liked Manny from our very first meeting. I was 34 and he was 54 with a very fatherly attitude towards me. He was a warm charismatic individual and very complimentary of my past accomplishments and said, "You are the answer to my prayers, as you are absolutely perfect for this job" (translation: You're the only qualified candidate stupid enough to apply). He was blind in one eye and sometimes, but not always, wore a black eye patch. Also, he often wore sandals and t-shirts which were never quite long enough to cover his slightly protruding belly exposing everyone to two or three inches of belly skin, not a pretty sight! Despite his appearance, I was very impressed with him; but in retrospect I had been taken in. To his credit, he had produced a number of notable movies including "Cabaret", "Papillion", "The Betsy" and "The Man Who Would Be King". Manny was a great story teller and would often talk about deception with a chuckle, a big smile and a twinkle in his eye when he said, "Come on in, the water is fine!" I soon discovered just how cold the water really was. (Read on, I'll explain more a little later.)

MANAGEMENT CONTRACTS

Before leaving an otherwise good top management position for another opportunity, you should insist on a management contract. I have always insisted on no more, or less, than a two-year contract. This guaranteed me that I would be paid my base pay for at least two years in the event that for whatever reason the new position did not work out. By the same token, two years is the maximum time that I would be willing to put up with a job that I disliked for any reason. If all goes well after two years, then no contract should be necessary as both parties will know each other well enough by that time, and you will always be free to leave when you wish. Only one of my three two-year contracts lasted for just two years. The other two contracts ended up lasting for 9 and 15 years.

My two-year employment contract with Apollo required that I would have full operational authority and a base pay plus 2% of the profits. Additionally, Apollo was to secure a minimum line of credit of two million dollars before I would be willing to tender my resignation at my current job. Manny assured me that he was finalizing the line of credit and wanted to hire me as soon as I could get there to turn the company around by whatever means possible.

A WOLF IN SHEEP'S CLOTHING

I left Apollo two months prior to the expiration of my two-year management contract due to a major problem with Manny Wolf. Despite the fact that my management contract stated that I was to receive 2% of the profits, which amounted to $40,000 on our $2,000,000 profit, Manny told me, "I can't legally pay you" (what the hell). Did I really hear him right? He went on to say, "Unfortunately, my hands are tied by Allied Artist's chapter 11 bankruptcy judge. The judge stipulated that for as long as Allied Artist was in chapter 11 that no one was to be paid more than X dollars which included any of its subsidiaries." Well, it just so happened that X dollars was exactly equal to my base pay! I asked him why he had entered into an agreement with me that he could not possibly have honored and he said, "I didn't think that anyone would have a snowball's chance in hell of turning the company around; so, I thought that it would be a non-issue". I sensed that he was being sincere, but I was incensed with his matter of fact cavalier attitude with absolutely no remorse whatsoever. Did this guy have a conscience, or what?

As I stood there speechless, I could see a slight hint of a sparkle in his good eye. I had seen that sparkle once before as he affectionately spoke of deception when he said, "Come on in the water is fine." I also detected a slight smirk on his face as if to say that he had outsmarted me. Still in a state of shock, I quickly pondered my options and said a short prayer as I calmly calculated the consequences of simply walking off the job.

I was absolutely outraged, to say the very least, but I knew that with two more months remaining on my management contract I couldn't just walk off the job, or could I? This was exactly what Apollo's prior president and management team had done two and a half years earlier. I have always subscribed to the practice of lining up your next job before quitting your current one, as a gap in employment raises a lot of questions from a prospective employer and badmouthing your prior employer never sounds good in an interview.

As the tension grew, Manny said that he knew that I would be a little upset (a little!) so he offered to pay me through the end of my contract if I wanted to resign. With the company now on good financial footing he probably felt that he no longer needed me and figured that he could run the company himself with the help of the excellent management team that I had assembled. He would later learn exactly where their loyalties resided.

Before I could respond to his offer, however, our heated conversation was interrupted by an urgent long distant phone call for me from New York. The caller was a man named Oscar Tang who said that he had been unsuccessfully trying to contact me for several days. Oscar said that he was the controlling shareholder of Executive Industries and asked if I would be interested in becoming the president of Executive Industries (prayer answered). Tom Frank had resigned as Executive's president and had highly recommended me as his replacement. I had worked for Tom as a vice president of Executive eight years earlier. I ended up resigning that day and was paid through the end of my contract.

I have often looked back on that day and I still can hardly believe the timing of Oscar's phone call and my subsequent good fortune.

I obviously learned that I should have reviewed not only the terms of Apollo's line of credit, but also Allied Artist's bankruptcy judge's rulings prior to going to work at Apollo. Additionally, I learned first hand what I had already known; namely, don't equate someone who is likeable to someone who is honest (easier said than done).

Interestingly enough, when I interviewed for the job with Oscar in New York he told me that he had actually met Manny (small world) and thought that he was an interesting character. Unbeknownst to me, Oscar said that Manny had come to his office trying to sell Apollo to Executive just six months earlier. Oscar then laughed and said, "I actually had to apologize to my business partner for allowing him in the building!" Oscar didn't elaborate but I could visualize the contrast between the Wall Street executives with their pin-stripped suits and Manny with his black eye patch, t-shirt and sandals. What I thought might have been a small hurdle turned out to be a nice walk in the park, as there were absolutely no credibility issues whatsoever regarding what I was telling Oscar about my experience with Manny. With tongue in cheek I said, "Oscar, you just need to get to know Manny a little better in order to love him as I do."

In retrospect, I believe that Manny had tried to sell Apollo while it was still extremely profitable before the conclusion of the Grumman contract. Even though Apollo's motor home manufacturing operations were profitable, I had estimated that its profitability would drop by over 50% after the conclusion of the Grumman contract, which was estimated to be wrapped-up within a year after Manny had met with Oscar. Manny may have been dishonest and deceptive but he was far from being stupid, especially when it came to money (his).

I will never be able to get inside Manny's head, nor do I want to, but I believe that his mindset relative to his appearance was that when you live in the Waldorf Astoria Hotel, you really don't need to "dress for success", as you have "already arrived". Other than letting everyone know where he lived, he certainly didn't put on any pretenses.

Were you wondering if I ever saw any signs along the way of Manny's character, or lack there of? Well, actually there were a few signs, like when we would go out to lunch and he would buy a Wall Street Journal from the coin operated newspaper rack, which was located at the front entrance to the restaurant. After inserting a coin he would swing open the security cover and remove "two" papers. He would always keep one for himself and then with a big smile hand the other one to me as a gift! He obviously didn't care what anyone thought, but it always made me feel a little uncomfortable. After the first couple of times I learned to distance myself while he was looting the newspaper rack. Even though I wasn't an accomplice, I always felt as if I were in possession of stolen goods until I rationalized that my copy was actually the one that he had purchased. His newspaper caper obviously didn't rise to the level of fraud.

There were, however, two major red flags; namely, the real reason for the abrupt defection of his prior management team and his difficulty in securing a legitimate line of credit. I never learned exactly why his past management team had abandoned him, but in retrospect it wouldn't be too difficult to speculate.

As to the financing, the fact that he had to go to people that he said he didn't respect and had concerns about their questionable character should have raised some flags. I simply discounted it due to the 21.5% prime interest rate and the tight credit markets at the time. One might have concluded that it was odd that a high profile well connected movie executive couldn't secure a more conventional line of credit, unless he had a bad reputation and had burned some bridges behind him. Since I didn't learn this information until two months after having quit my job as a vice president of a competing company, I had already **"crossed the Rubicon"**. (Crossing the Rubicon River was **the point of no return** for Julius Caesar and his army as they were in defiance of Pompey's orders, which was an act of treason that led to a civil war and the beginning of the Roman Empire.)

I had resigned my prior job in good standing; however, the owner/president, Ottie, was none too pleased that I was leaving to run a competing company. There was absolutely no going back. Even though Ottie had offered me my boss's position to stay, I refused to stab him in the back. I never told my boss of Ottie's offer, so he was in no way, shape or form indebted to me; however, two years later it was his excellent job reference regarding my character that helped me secure the job with Executive Industries. Nothing good ever comes from betrayal, but much good will always come from your good character.

Michael Hill

TO HATE OR NOT TO HATE?

It is easier said than done, but harboring hatred or resentment only harms you, so get over it and move on with your life.

My initial instinct was to sue Manny personally for fraud but I became so involved in my job at Executive Industries that I never did. I did take great satisfaction in that not only had my loyal management team, which I had assembled at Apollo, follow me to Executive, but within three years Apollo had closed its doors. It was never my intention to attempt to put them out of business, as there were a lot of good people that would lose their jobs and it should never be anyone's objective; but, with Manny at the helm, it was just a matter of time. In retrospect, I felt that I knew why Apollo's previous top management team had all walked off the job the same day without notice. Maybe his failure at Allied Artist was less about bad movies and more about bad karma!

My feelings toward Manny were not good, to say the very least, but I believe that it is better to dislike someone than to be disliked, so always think twice before suing someone. Essentially, you can control your own feelings and hopefully overcome negative thoughts. However, you will never be able to control the feelings of others and you never know how they will react towards you if you take action against them.

Fortunately, I was able to convince myself that if my experience with Manny was going to be the worst thing to ever happen to me in my life, then I would be pretty lucky, which I have been. In retrospect, I was also happy that I had not negotiated for 10% of Apollo's profits, as being cheated out of $200,000 would have been a lot more difficult to walk away from.

"Resentment is like drinking poison and hoping it will kill your enemies." Nelson Mandela

KNOW YOUR PROSPECTIVE EMPLOYER

After leaving Apollo, I had two great opportunities to either become president of Revcon or Executive Industries. Some acquaintances in the industry advised me not to take the Revcon job, as it was rumored that the owner was in the Mafia. Wow, this was the third time that I was hearing about the Mafia. Prior to my interview with Dale Gustafson, the owner of Revcon, I was told that he had fallen out of favor with the Mafia and consequently had lost his left arm, but he reportedly had told everyone that he lost his arm in a boating accident. I interviewed with him, and sure enough, he was a one armed owner, but what was the truth? Dale and I hit it off great in the interview and, since he knew a lot more about me than I did of him, he made me an offer on the spot. Since I had already booked a flight to New York the following week to interview for the Executive Industry job, I told him that I would let him know when I returned to California. He said fine, but added that if things didn't go well in New York that I should stop in on my way back to California to see him in Minneapolis, Minnesota, where he said he owned several banks.

The Executive job interview went very well with Oscar Tang; so, when he made me an offer I accepted it. I knew Executive Industries very well as I had been the Vice President of Operations for Executive eight years prior, hence Oscar had actively recruited me. Oscar was the controlling shareholder of Executive Industries, a public company, and a billionaire who co-founded Reich and Tang, a New York investment company. Oscar told me that he was born in Shanghai, China and in 1949 when the Communists came into power; his father moved their textile business to Hong Kong. After relocating to Hong Kong he had purchased a large plot of land for his textile business, which they subsequently sold for $250,000,000. Oscar was educated in the United States and received an engineering degree from Yale and his MBA from Harvard.

If my interview with Oscar had not gone well then I was prepared to follow up on Dale's offer; his ownership of several banks really intrigued me, especially as credit lines were still extremely tight. Well, six months after starting my job at Executive I read an article in the Los Angeles Times which reported that Dale Gustafson had been indicted on charges of check kiting between his banks in Minnesota and the Tropicana Hotel & Casino in Las Vegas where he held an ownership interest. He was sentenced to federal prison and was required to divest his ownership interest in the Tropicana. Two years later, while still in prison, he had heard of our success at Executive; so, he had his "left-hand man" contact me with another offer, which I respectfully declined. I obviously learned that I should have performed a background check on him but I dodged the proverbial bullet anyway.

It was a great eight-year run as president of Executive at which time I sold the company for Oscar and moved on to my next job at Rexhall Industries.

DON'T RISK LOSING GOOD EMPLOYEES

I had always assumed that anyone who observed my work ethic would realize that I was doing something important for the company. It was my boss' responsibility and duty to recognize and appreciate my contribution to the company. Okay, I have a high opinion of my worth, but then again, I was always the first to arrive at the office in the morning and usually the last one to leave. Throughout my career I never had to ask for a raise because my contribution and worth had generally been recognized, appreciated, and generously rewarded.

If you are an ambitious overachiever who has proven his or her worth and your employer does not acknowledge it, then you are working for the wrong company.

Acknowledgement can take a number of forms, should it be a pat on the back, a raise or a promotion. It is your boss' responsibility to the company to bring along the best and the brightest employees. You should not have to ask for a raise. In fact, your employer should be concerned that you may leave if they don't give you a raise or promotion. If you need to ask, then you are probably working for the wrong company.

During my first two years as Vice President of Rexhall Industries, a publicly owned company, the company had been losing money, but it was cash rich due to an IPO (Initial Public Offering) a year before I joined the company. For those unfamiliar with an IPO, an IPO is the process of taking a private company public. In other words, a privately owned company will sell a portion of its shares or stock to the public. The funds raised are reflected on the company's books as equity and not as debt; therefore, the funds become additional working capital, which never has to be paid back and bears no interest expense. It is debt free money, which helps companies grow without the burden of a heavy debt load and the associated interest expense. Furthermore, after "going public" the company has an ongoing fiduciary responsibility to all shareholders, as the total of all its shareholders represents the ownership of the company.

During that two-year period of losses, I was promised 4% of the company's future pre-tax profits if I could help turn the business around, which of course was a great incentive. I embraced a percentage of the profits because Rexhall was a public company and I was in charge of overseeing the accounting department, so I knew that we would be generating accurate income statements to be released to our public shareholders.

Rexhall manufactured a variety of vehicles, but no one, including the CFO, knew which vehicles were profitable and which were not. Since we needed to return the company back to profitability, I terminated the CFO, who was a CPA making $115,000 per year, and personally accepted the added responsibility of CFO at no additional compensation for a net savings to the company. This was an exciting challenge and great experience, as I would now be personally generating 10-Q's (Quarterly financial statements) and 10-K's (Annual financial statements) per SEC (Security Exchange Commission) regulations for distribution to our public shareholders. These additional duties also included being the chairperson at its annual shareholder's meeting. A lot of extra work was required but I found it to be very educational and rewarding, as I quickly became intimate with the inter workings of the financial heartbeat of the company, which gave me incredible insight into its cost structures.

Next, after a comprehensive cost analysis, I proved to Bill Rex, the president and founder, that one of the vehicles, the Vision, was costing the company more to produce than its selling price; so, I recommended discontinuing it immediately. I could hardly believe my ears when he said, "Mike, I can't discontinue the Vision because it is not only our best selling product but I personally hyped it to the stockbrokers last year as the main reason why we needed the six million dollar IPO for its product development, production tooling and marketing."

Bill clearly understood that if we were losing money on every sale we weren't going to make up for it with volume. In fact, the more successful the product became the more money we lost. It was only a best seller because it was way under priced. Since I clearly understood Bill's dilemma, I suggested that we increase the price substantially and let it die a natural death, which it did. I also informed him that the company's shareholders were only interested in one thing and that was the increase in the company's stock price, as they couldn't care less how we accomplished it.

Bill's genius was in product development; so, he quickly developed new vehicles which I helped cost and price at profitable margins.

My second two years saw the company slowly return to profitability. The company's shareholders were extremely happy, as Rexhall's stock price had quadrupled in value. Unfortunately, two years after the company had returned to profitability my 4% incentive was withdrawn just as we were on track to making upwards of $4,000,000 in pre-tax profits. Bill defended his decision by telling me that he had not guaranteed that my 4% was going to last forever! He was absolutely correct, so despite voicing my great displeasure I essentially sucked it up, said a short prayer, and calmed down.

Since Bill's personal income, which included 10% of the pre-profits, continued to increase every month with our ever increasing profitability, I realized that he embraced a **philosophy**

of scarcity in that the less he paid me the more he would make for himself; but it was a philosophy that was short lived, at least as far as I was concerned. Bill was an honest straightforward person, however, I felt that after all of my hard work, dedication and demonstrated worth that he was not being fair; hence, I lost my desire to work for him despite otherwise loving my job.

This was a totally different situation than I had encountered with Manny Wolf twelve years earlier. In Manny's case <u>I had learned not to equate someone who is likeable to someone who is honest.</u> In this case <u>I learned not to equate someone who is honest to someone who is fair.</u> I had always thought of them as being one in the same (big mistake).

Another difference was that this time there was no phone saving call while Bill was informing me of his decision; however, several weeks later, before I could get my job search underway, I received an important phone call. The phone call was from an insurance broker named Chuck Fosdick, whom I had done a favor for several years earlier. Chuck asked how Rexhall was doing and I said it was doing great but that I was dissatisfied and interested in looking for other business opportunities. Chuck seemed a little excited and said, "I underwrite the insurance for a guy who really needs your talents but he doesn't know it yet. Let me talk to him and I'll get back to you."

Several months later Chuck introduced me to Ed Grech, the owner of Krystal Enterprises, the world's largest manufacturer of stretched limousines.

Even though I continued to be the second highest paid at Rexhall, after Bill's action I never felt a real sense of security; so, several months later, after four and a half years of service, I left Rexhall to pursue what turned out to be a great 15-year career with Ed Grech at Krystal Enterprises as Vice President of Operations and CFO (prayer answered). Bill was very upset when I resigned but he was somewhat pleased when I told him that I was not going to work for a competitor. I will never know why Bill was so short sighted but I did take satisfaction in knowing that he hired two people to replace me, a Vice President of Operations and a CFO.

Chuck was a very nice guy and when I thanked him for his efforts in introducing and recommending me to Ed he said, "Mike, no need for any thanks, I was actually doing Ed a favor, not you." Wow, what a great sentiment from a classy guy. It is interesting how a favor that you never have any expectations of being returned somehow comes back to you when you need it the most ("what goes around comes around").

In contrast to Bill, Ed embraced a **philosophy of abundance** whereby the more he paid me the more he would make, and he was right. Even though Ed placed an annual salary cap on my compensation package, it was set high enough at $1,000,000 that I quickly began earning four times what I had been paid at Rexhall. The compensation was a great incentive, however my greatest motivation was in the challenge of doing my job to the best of my ability; if I did that then I knew that both the money and job security would automatically follow. During my first four years we grew the company from $30,000,000 in annual sales to over $140,000,000!

Ed was not only both honest and fair, but he was also generous to a fault (a fault that I could easily live with). He certainly knew how to build company loyalty by spreading the wealth.

The bottom line is that in order to keep good employees you must treat them fairly, recognize their worth and compensate them accordingly. Don't be "Penny wise and pound foolish".

"TRY" IS ONE OF THE WORST WORDS EVER

Always watch out for people who say they will "try". This is a word that should never be used as it invites misinterpretation. More often than not, when people tell you they will "try", what they are really saying is that they will "only try", and in no way shape or form are they actually committing themselves to accomplishing the task. I have learned to never accept an answer that someone will "try", and I make it clear that "trying" is not an acceptable response. If you want something done, then get a 100% commitment. If you don't make this clear from the outset, then when things don't get done you will be reminded that they only said that they would "try" to do it.

Unfortunately, some people don't hear the word "try" and proceed with the false impression that someone will actually do something. Don't set yourself up for disappointment by not understanding exactly what people are saying. Conversely, never tell someone that you will try to do something because if you end up not doing it, you will leave the impression that you either tried but failed, or simply blew the task off with no intention of ever really doing it in the first place. Since there is nothing to be gained and everything to lose, remove the word "try" from your vocabulary.

KEEPING YOUR PROMISE

If you make a promise or a commitment, make sure to keep it. But if for reasons outside of your control it is not possible to do so, don't make the mistake of informing the other party after the fact. Instead, once you have the knowledge that the commitment will be impossible to keep, immediately inform the other party of the problem. If you don't, you will have failed because you prevent the other party from doing something to mitigate the situation like going to the person who is in control. Simply put, don't leave people hanging, even on items that you may regard as minor, as letting people down on even minor items will tell them a lot about you.

TAKE RESPONSIBILITY FOR YOUR MISTAKES

It is human nature to automatically blame others for our own failings either consciously or subconsciously. This is self destructive because by doing so you alienate those whom you wrongfully blame and inhibit your own growth as a person. When you do this you are basically in complete denial of the truth. Your ego will not allow you to take the blame or accept responsibility and therefore it is always someone else's fault. Be honest with yourself, which is not always easy. I have found that it is easier for people to be mad at someone else as one's ego is such a fragile thing. I believe this is because it is easier for us to forgive others than to forgive ourselves. Sometimes we can be very hard on ourselves and in some cases we can be our own worst enemy.

"I didn't say it was your fault, I said I was blaming you." Anonymous

"My only mistake was in thinking that I had made a mistake when, in fact, I actually hadn't." Anonymous

VIOLATION OF CONFIDENCE

If you violate a confidence, it will come back to haunt you. Unfortunately, this is a lesson that, more often than not, is learned the hard way. Just because you think you know where someone's loyalty and self-interest lie, don't assume that your request for confidentiality will be honored or that they will even commit to it. After all, if you can't keep your own secrets, how do you expect others to do so?

The number-one reason why people in business violate confidences is because they present themselves as persons in the know with great contacts; it makes them feel more important. Another more nefarious reason is that they are playing politics by trying to undermine your position. Don't be either of these people. It can ruin your career.

While I was a vice president of a company during an economic downturn the president suspended year-end raises and cancelled everyone's Christmas bonus just prior to the end of the year. This led to a deterioration of employee morale as most of the employees were counting on their bonus to purchase Christmas presents. Shortly after announcing this policy change another vice president informed me that the president had just purchased a new Ferrari for $250,000 while on vacation. My response was that I hoped he would know not to bring it to work as it would not be appropriate in light of our new austerity program and he agreed. Well, about an hour later I received a nasty phone call from the president asking me who the hell I thought I was by saying that he should not bring his new car to work. Wow, what a great conversation! This event didn't ruin my relationship with the president, but it sure hurt my relationship with the associate who violated my confidence. I should have kept my thoughts to myself until I had an opportunity to speak directly to the president about my concerns.

AVOIDING EMPLOYEE LAWSUITS

The backstabbing vice president in the preceding story, whom I will refer to as Dick, had a nasty abusive attitude towards the company's employees. He had always expressed his negative intolerant feelings verbally; however, on one occasion he actually got so angry that he physically attacked one of the company's employees and then fired him. Immediately afterwards the employee came to my office with two witnesses to explain how he had been physically attacked and begged for his job back. Sensing a potential assault and battery lawsuit I quickly calmed him down by telling him that there was no need for me to rehire him because he had never been fired in the first place. I informed him that Dick could not fire him without first following the company's proper protocol of going through the Human Resources Department. Further, I told him that I would take appropriate action to ensure that this type of behavior would never happen again. He was extremely relieved as he thanked me and left my office.

I immediately informed the president of what had happened which was easily verified during our subsequent investigation. It was absolutely incumbent upon the company to take corrective action for legal reasons. Documenting the fact that the company had taken this matter very seriously by taking appropriate action to prevent this type of behavior from ever happening again would go a long way in a court of law if the employee ever decided to file suit claiming an ongoing hostile work environment. **Employers must provide a safe work environment and employees must clearly understand that any behavior that may lead to a hostile work environment will absolutely not be tolerated.**

If Dick had worked for me I would have fired him. Even though the president did not fire him, he did agree to order him to attend an Anger Management Class on a Saturday, as doing nothing was clearly not an option.

After Dick reluctantly agreed to give up his precious Saturday to attend an eight-hour class, I could hardly wait until Monday to ask him how it had gone and if he had learned anything. Dick's response was absolutely priceless, "It was a total waste of time. How would you like spending your entire Saturday with a room full of nothing but F-ing assholes?" (Obviously there were no exceptions)

The employee never sued the company but we did protect the company from a potential lawsuit by documenting our action despite the obvious ineffectiveness of the Anger Management Class.

NEVER CLASSIFY YOUR FRIENDS BY RACE, CREED OR RELIGION

Your friends are your friends, period. In conversations, don't make the subtle mistake of referring to your friends as Jewish friends, African American friends, Hispanic friends, Asian friends, etc. If you happen to be white, you wouldn't refer to your friends as being your white friends any more than a Jewish person would refer to his or her friends as being Jewish friends. This may seem obvious, however, I have often heard people say that they have Jewish friends, African American friends etc. It is nice that they have a diversified group of friends, but to classify them in this manner is an offensive qualification. If you ever make reference to your ethnic friends, then just refer to them as your friends without distinction, period. If you feel that it is necessary for someone to know that you are multicultural, then simply refer to your good friend as being your friend, who just happens to be Jewish, African American, or whatever.

Michael Hill

CHAPTER 5

PROVEN TECHNIQUES FOR SUCCESS

Michael Hill

BECOME A CHEERLEADER

The best way to be an effective leader is to be supportive of your employees. It means sharing credit when credit is due. It means praising your employees every chance you get, provided it is sincere and deserved.

Once while giving a plant tour I praised an employee in front of our customers for his attention to detail. The employee had not been doing a very good job previously and I was genuinely pleased that he was showing signs of improvement. From that day forward not only did that employee's job performance improve but also every time I was in the plant he made a point of showing me how he had come up with new ideas for product improvement. Noticing his quality of work and praising him, especially in front of others, gave him a tremendous amount of pride in his job. Multiply this by just one employee per day for fifty-two weeks per year and just see what a difference it will make. You will not only see an improvement in efficiencies and quality but also an incredible improvement in your relationship with your employees.

Positive feedback not only reinforces good behavior but it also satisfies the insatiable human need to enhance one's self-image. In fact, feedback, especially from top management, is extremely valuable even if it is about something relatively small. Unfortunately, I have often found that top management either didn't understand the importance of giving positive feedback or simply felt that it was beneath them.

Essentially, you will need to be a cheerleader of sorts. <u>Make a habit of giving positive feedback to at least one employee every day</u>. It should become a habit. If you don't have employees that deserve praise, then you either don't have the ability to recognize good performance or you have the wrong employees. Reprimands are also necessary when needed and will allow a failing employee to take corrective action. It would be unfair to fire someone for poor performance if you have not first given them proper warning along the way. One of the most difficult jobs for a manager is firing someone. I have learned that by keeping your employees well informed about their performance and by giving them recommendations of how they can improve their performance makes the unpleasant task of firing someone somewhat easier and less frequent.

THINKING OUTSIDE THE BOX

In the academic world there is a saying regarding professors, "Publish or Perish". I have learned that the equivalent in the business world is that you must be flexible, creative and innovative, or fail. By thinking outside the box you will force yourself to be flexible, creative and innovative. Flexible in terms of being willing to rethink past business practices in a creative way in order to best serve your customers, and innovative in terms of implementing creative ideas. This is a never-ending process that drives both your sales and your company's success. You can never rest on your laurels, as your competitors will always be competing for your customers.

Creativity must be converted to innovation for it to be of value. Having failures is a learning process and you will find that you will learn far more from your failures than from your successes; at least that has been the case in my life. Never let your failures stop you; otherwise you will have failed. As the saying goes, "Quitters never win and winners never quit".

"If we all went to business school and learned about past business practices, then we would all be reading by candle light, as conventional thinking stifles innovation." Thomas Edison

---

First I will give you an example of what not to do. While working for The Leisure Group at its facilities in Pine Bluff, Arkansas I witnessed what I will call **"the arrogance of**

inflexibility". I was the acting operations manager for its backpack manufacturing company, which I had moved there from California. Our sister company at the facilities was the Ben Pearson Archery company world famous for its bows made of exotic woods from around the world, like rose wood from Africa. The bows were absolutely beautiful and were only matched by its performance worldwide with the heralded escapades of big game hunter, Jim Dougherty, who became a legend for taking down big game with just a bow and arrow. His numerous accomplishments coupled with his endorsement of Ben Pearson bows made the product line the undisputed leader in its field.

Well, in the early seventies there was a new revolutionary bow that was entering the market, a bow that looked down right stupid at the time. It was the advent of the compound bow that ended up revolutionizing the industry. Because of its dull fiberglass appearance and strange mechanical pulleys, the Ben Pearson executives just laughed it off as being a stupid idea.

Unfortunately for The Leisure Group, the compound bow took off like a wild fire in just a few years. Except for a few purists, most of the big game hunters switched over to compound bows because it was simply a superior product; it was shorter making it easier to navigate the underbrush without getting the bow hung up and it had a great mechanical advantage. With just 25 pounds of pull it could deliver the same power as the company's 50-pound bows! This was a tremendous innovation since the lesser the amount of pull the greater the capability to not only keep the bow steadier but the arrow could more easily be held for much longer periods of time without fatigue, affording time for the optimal shot. It required several ownership changes before the company finally developed its own compound bow.

Now I will switch to the correct mindset. In the early stages of my 15-year limousine-manufacturing days the company's customers were expressing an increasing interest in being able to move more passengers by purchasing small buses; but we also learned that they were dissatisfied with the quality of those buses both in terms of workmanship and aesthetic design. The mid-sized bus industry's somewhat crude mind-set at the time was that the mid-sized buses or shuttle busses were "butt movers" and that their objective was simply to move as many butts as possible at the lowest cost per butt. Conversely, we recognized that our limousine customers had a totally different mind-set for their higher profile clientele who were willing to pay more to travel in luxury. They desired higher quality craftsmanship and a smoother ride with aesthetically pleasing designs, which is what they were accustomed to with our limousines. Consequently, my first major project at Krystal Enterprises was to enter the bus manufacturing industry by creating a bus to meet our customer's needs. Despite being a higher priced product, we took the mid-sized bus industry by storm and set new industry standards for quality. After just four years the new bus product line was responsible for half of the company's sales, which helped triple its profits. The GSA (General Services Administration) embraced our bus and actually wrote their government bus bid specifications based on our bus. This allowed us to sell our buses to the NSA (National Security Agency), the FBI, Fort Knox and a whole host of air force bases around the country. Anyone who wished to bid against our bus was required to meet our high standard of quality specifications, which kept us from being undercut by an inferior less costly bus. Additionally, we expanded our bus business by selling mobile command centers and prisoner transport buses to law enforcement agencies across the country.

Another example is in the case of a matchbox manufacturer. The CEO was extremely dismayed to discover that an unacceptable number of complaints were being received regarding empty matchboxes shipped to customers. He immediately contracted with a consulting firm and for one million dollars a state of the art electronic scale was installed at the end of the conveyor belt assembly line, which would alert the plant of an empty box. In fact, not only would the plant be alerted via a loud bell and the shutting down of the conveyor belt, but also a daily report would be sent directly to the CEO's office computer. Well, for the first two weeks the CEO received reports indicating that the system was working very well as a significant number of matchboxes were being rejected as empty. Mission accomplished, so he thought, but after another two weeks he noticed from his reports that zero boxes were being rejected; this made no sense. The only way this could happen is if either the expensive system was no longer working or somehow the production line became error free, which was impossible. Being totally baffled, he decided to pay a visit to the plant. Upon his inspection he noticed that a fan had been installed at the end of the assembly line and that there were a number of empty boxes lying on the floor. Still somewhat bewildered, he asked the production supervisor what was going on and was informed that the production workers were sick and tired of having to run to the end of the assembly line to restart the conveyor belt every time the bell rang; so, they installed a $30 fan as the solution!

A company for which I was a vice president had grown its business so fast that it exceeded its VOC (Volatile Organic Compound) limit as allocated by the AQMD (Air Quality Management District). The company didn't just exceed it but rather shattered it by 120%, more than twice its allocated limit.

The AQMD has an incredible amount of power and authority as mandated by the Federal Clear Air Bill under the EPA (Environmental Protection Agency). It regulates and enforces compliance according to federally mandated guidelines for the state. Hence, the AQMD has the power not only to assess fines but also to shut down companies found to be noncompliant.

The company had been growing so fast that management was unaware that it had exceeded its VOC limit. The company's IT Department was responsible for complying with the AQMD reporting requirements, which included both quarterly and annual reporting of its VOC usage, but the department was spread so thin due to the company's rapid growth that it failed to raise any warning flags. The department did however do an excellent job of accurately reporting the company's VOC usage to the AQMD and in a timely manner. This was by no means an easy task for the IT department as the VOC calculations were extremely complex. The company's noncompliance had continued for well over a year before an AQMD compliance officer conducting a routine inspection issued the company a citation.

Not only could the fine for the citation be in the tens of thousands of dollars but also the AQMD could potentially shut down the company for such an egregious violation. A week later the company received a fine for $150,000 and was informed that it was required to comply immediately or face a $2,500 per day fine for every day going forward that it was not in full compliance. In order to immediately come into compliance, the company would be required to cut production by 55% which would require laying off 250 employees and wiping out the company's profit margin at that reduced level. Yes, just another stress free day at the factory! What to do?

I immediately consulted with George Jaramillo, the company's "really smart" corporate attorney and good friend. He explained that per Federal law the AQMD was responsible for overseeing and regulating companies in its district to ensure absolute compliance. Even though the company had not lied on the AQMD reports and had actually self-incriminated itself via the reports, he went on to say that ignorance of having violated the law was obviously no excuse for breaking the law; however, our honesty was going to save the day and he had the perfect strategy. Wow, but how?

Well, George informed the AQMD that they were "derelict if not complicit" for actually allowing the company to be out of compliance considering the company had been reporting its noncompliance in writing to them for well over a year. The AQMD had simply not done its job to ensure that the company was fully compliant as required by the Federal government and were, in fact, in violation of its Federal mandate. We were outraged (absolutely)!

The bottom line was that the fine was reduced to zero and the AQMD allowed the company an entire year to get back into full compliance without being fined in the process which proved to be just enough time to upgrade the company's equipment for a substantial VOC emissions reduction. (I subsequently upgraded George from "really smart" to "brilliant")

Giving a thief the keys to your business is not only counter intuitive, but also sounds down right stupid; however, that is exactly what the owner/president, Ottie Alburn, of a company I worked for actually did!

While I was Vice President of Operations of Vogue Coach we had a theft problem and we were almost 100% certain that the culprit was one of our most valuable production supervisors whom I will refer to as Jose. After a lengthy discussion with Ottie about the termination of this valued employee, he made a startling statement, "Let's give him a promotion with a raise and give him the keys to the facility, but make it clear to him that we expect him to secure the company's assets and lock-up every night as part of his new responsibilities." Jose ended up doing a great job; and we never lost anything after that day, go figure!

Ottie was a very interesting guy to say the least. He was a laid back musician who played a mean horn for well known bands during the big band era such as the Glen Miller Band and Les Brown's Band of Renown. In Ottie's wisdom of providing the keys to our suspected thief I came to realize that Jose would know that he would either be blamed for a lack of security, or be considered a prime suspect if items went missing. Also, giving him a raise made the risk of losing his job not worth it. As crazy as it may seem, I believe that Jose was so impressed with our faith in him that he did not want to let us down. In fact, I noticed a positive change in his demeanor; he actually became more friendly and helpful. In any event, we kept our most valuable supervisor, which proved to be critical to my production plans and to the company's future growth.

While waiting to attend graduate school in the fall of 1968, I accepted a summer job in a management-training program with

Procter & Gamble at its terminal annex manufacturing facility in Long Beach, California. As a warehouse supervisor, I supervised longshoremen in all warehouse operations ranging from unloading rail cars of products shipped from other P&G manufacturing plants to the warehousing and shipping of its products to hundreds of stores in California and Hawaii.

After a couple of weeks, my boss, John Houston, challenged me to discover a less costly way to determine the <u>average weight</u> of each of its products, which were periodically being weighed in compliance with Weights and Measures Standards. He told me that the weighing process was a very time consuming and costly process. He then said, "If you can figure this out, then you will be a P&G hero."

I thought his use of the word "hero" was very strange at the time; years later however, I learned that P&G had a philosophy of embracing a socialization process of making brand managers believe that they were heroes. It sounds a little strange, but it is a big part of P&G's success. This is an ego driven process to make their managers believe that they are empowered. If you feel good about yourself, then it is a great motivator for you to excel as a problem solver, or in P&G's case, a hero.

As strange as it may seem, I have learned that other top rated companies have their own "hero" status recognition; Wal-Mart uses "Associate", McDonald's "Crew Member" and Disney "Cast Member".

I was pleased with John's faith in me; yet I didn't feel that it was well founded, as I didn't have a clue as to what to do; therefore, I simply focused on doing my job of supervising the warehouse employees. The warehouse was a high paced operation with a tremendous product turnover; 40-foot trailers and MATSON seagoing cargo containers were being loaded from twelve loading docks on two shifts 16 hours per day. Even though we inventoried over 100 products, most shipments were comprised of no more than about 24 different products from Crisco oil to Crest toothpaste, but in different quantities of each product, no two trailers or containers were ever loaded the same.

About a week later while consolidating bills of lading it dawned on me that each trailer and container had been weighed on our truck scale having generated a weight ticket representing the net shipping weight of the loaded trailer or container. The net shipping weight is the total weight less the weight of the empty trailer or container having been weighed prior to being loaded. In other words, the weight tickets represented the total net weight of the products being shipped in every trailer or cargo container. This was an interesting observation but how was it useful?

Well, after several days of consciously and subconsciously pondering John's challenge, I realized that the solution was quite simple and John was extremely pleased with my subsequent analysis. In fact, two years later, after receiving my graduate degrees, he offered me an excellent job at P&G; however, I elected to go to work for The Leisure Group.

Now for the solution: you will remember from your algebra class that if you have one unknown, then you need only one equation to solve for the value of the unknown. Likewise, if you have two unknowns then you will need two equations to solve for the values of the two unknowns. Consequently, if you have 24 unknowns, then you will need 24 equations to solve for the value of the 24 unknowns.

The solution required the creation of the same number of equations as the number of different products being shipped. In our case it usually meant 24 equations with 24 unknowns, which required weight tickets from 24 shipments. Each equation was then created to equal the net weight of the products being shipped.

As a simple example, consider three shipments of varying quantities of three different products being shipped with a net weight according to the bill of lading weight ticket for each of the respective three shipments as follows (three unknowns, therefore three equations):

10 boxes of Ivory + 20 cans of Crisco + 15 boxes of Tide = 255 lbs
3 boxes of Ivory + 5 cans of Crisco + 8 boxes of Tide = 77 lbs
7 boxes of Ivory + 15 cans of Crisco + 20 boxes of Tide = 217 lbs

Each of the three shipments in the example above is represented in the following equations with X being the weight of a box of Ivory soap, Y being the weight of a can of Crisco and Z being the weight of a box of Tide:

$10X + 20Y + 15Z = 255$ pounds
$3X + 5Y + 8Z = 77$ pounds
$7X + 15Y + 20Z = 217$ pounds

Solving for X, Y and Z we get the following values:
$X = 1$ pound per box of Ivory soap
$Y = 10$ pounds per can of Crisco
$Z = 3$ pounds per box of Tide

Just as I had learned in "Lemons to Lemonade", sometimes a solution to a problem often turned out to be so good that I wondered why it hadn't been thought of previously. The best ideas are only limited by our ability to think creatively.

In 1972 I was a vice president of a leading luxury motor home manufacturer when GM (General Motors) announced its entry into the luxury motor home market. GM's motor home was absolutely beautiful with its sleek clean exterior lines. According to its annual report it had spent $2,100,000 over a two year period making match-mold dies to mass-produce its sleek low profile almost seamless aluminum and fiberglass bodies for both a 23 and 26 foot motor home; the two most popular sizes at that time. It also stated that the motor homes were being priced to be very competitive and its durable tooling and massive facilities would allow for production of up to 20,000 vehicles per year. At that level of production GM clearly wanted to capture a major percentage of the luxury motor home market, which could only be possible by putting others out of business; us included!

Even though there was always a certain amount of "evolutionary" innovations in the industry every year, the GM motor home was absolutely "revolutionary". Since our company had always shared relatively the same strengths and weaknesses as its direct competitors, the common and basic competitive strategy utilized was to have pricing wars; but what do we do to compete against such a superior GM product?

We were very concerned about this giant entering the luxury motor home market to say the least. We viewed it as a David and Goliath situation whereby we needed to quickly assess our strengths versus their weaknesses in order to survive. Since GM was locked into just two sizes of motor homes (23 and 26 foot), due to the long tooling lead-time and high tooling costs, we saw this as GM's biggest weakness; namely, **a lack of flexibility**. We quickly started producing larger 28, 30, 33 and even 35-foot models with greater utility value for not much more money. These new models became very popular and all of our competitors, except GM, quickly started manufacturing these larger motor homes. Additionally, our company's breakeven point was very low and the new models required zero tooling costs since the bodies were constructed by laminating aluminum to prefabricated wood framed walls; hence, a tremendous flexibility in making different length vehicles very quickly with a large variety of optional floor plans. The GM motor homes were far superior as touring vehicles, due to its custom designed chassis, but its compact floor plan designs were far from superior for actually camping.

After three years GM was only selling 2,500 vehicles annually, which was equal to our sales, but our lower overhead allowed us to make a nice profit whereas GM was losing serious money due to its huge overhead costs ("large economy of scale"). Consequently, GM exited the industry three years later in 1978 after only building a grand total of about 13,000 vehicles over the course of six years; a far cry from 20,000 vehicles per year!

There is another important lesson here; if you have a competitor that is a public company, then make sure to obtain as much public information about that company as possible i.e. Press Releases and Quarterly & Annual Reports.

One of the best "outside the box" thinkers I know is Jim Rolph, a Mensa member. Jim was my Chief Engineer at three companies and he also taught my wife to water ski, which was very interesting as she is right/left challenged. He quickly learned that she was having a problem when she looked confused when he told her to put her left foot forward on the ski. Well, Jim had the perfect solution, "Lynne, your left foot is the one with the big toe on the right!" Yes, he certainly had a great sense of humor. Seriously, I credit him with a lot of the success in my career, as he is great at product development and an excellent hands-on problem solver not to mention a real joy to work with. He truly is a Renaissance man.

Jim would often remind me that, "Form follows function"; but, if we didn't like the form, then his genius was in tweaking the design to make it more aesthetically pleasing. Even though beauty is a subjective observation, there was usually a consensus as to whether or not the design aspects were pleasing. In Jim's words, "Beauty may only be skin deep, but ugly goes all the way to the bone." Masking over the mandatory aspects of a design's form is an "art form" and no one did it better than Jim. He once redesigned a Sprinter van, which was so impressive that everyone thought that it should have looked the way he redesigned it when it left the Sprinter factory. In all modesty, Jim would often say, "The first guy never has a chance", as improving on someone else's design was always easy, at least for him. Surrounding yourself with talented people, like Jim, is one of the most important keys to success.

One of my favorite stories is about a man who gets a flat tire just outside an insane asylum; and, while changing the tire he accidentally kicks the hubcap containing all of the lug nuts into the storm drain. Totally demoralized and distraught he sat down on the curb and started crying. His crying was loud enough to attract the attention of one of the patients who came to the fence and tried to console him. Well, after a short period of time they struck up a friendship and the patient tries to convince the man that if he would help him get out, he had a solution to his tire dilemma. The man eventually agreed and after getting him over the fence the guy proceeded to make good on his promise; however, when he removed the other three hubcaps the man started questioning his own judgment in letting this crazy guy out. Well, to his amazement the guy then removed one lug nut from each of the other three wheels and proceeded to use them to secure the spare tire!

Absolutely flabbergasted, the man asks the guy why he was in the asylum since it was obvious that he wasn't crazy. In response the guy said, "I may be crazy, but I am not stupid!"

"There is a thin line between genius and insanity. I have erased that line." Oscar Levant

---

Don't be discouraged if you find yourself going down the wrong path. I often found myself going down blind alleys; the good news was that it always eliminated a lot of bad possibilities. I was never discouraged because I had become accustomed to wrong answers ever since the age of 14. It all started with a number of the wrong answers to mathematical problems prior to finding the correct one. Eliminating all of the wrong answers was a great learning process because once the correct answer was apparent, I could appreciate it on a totally different level than many of my fellow students who solved the problem on their first attempt. The insight that I gained from the wrong answers was a better understanding of why it was wrong. This in turn gave me a greater appreciation for the process that resulted in the correct one. The number of wrong answers that I could generate always amazed me; it was mindboggling (I was actually living outside the box while trying to get in)! The upside, however, was two fold, it gave me a tenacious attitude, and once I understood the correct path, I truly understood it inside and out. The bottom line is that by experimenting you will make a lot of mistakes but experimentation is an extremely important tool for success. Sometimes even the wrong answer can be a success, i.e. 3M's Post-Its (the glue did not have enough holding power for its intended purpose, so 3M employees started using it to post notes to documents).

"I have not failed. I've just found 10,000 ways that won't work." Thomas Edison

---

I don't purport to know how to teach someone to think outside the box, however, I have found that by not forcing a solution, but rather letting your sub-conscience mind ponder possible solutions is sometimes the best approach. Daydreaming doesn't seem like it would be very productive but I have found it to be productive on a number of occasions. As a cautionary note, it is best not to try this at work as it could very easily be confused with goofing off!!

Another tool that I found to be very useful was to use a "3D space visualization" technique. I first learned this technique in a mechanical engineering drafting class. In order to draw a mechanical engineering drawing of a three-dimensional object you must first draw the object from the three basic perspectives of front, top and side view. Since the object also has a back, bottom and an opposite side, it is necessary for you to "see through" or visualize the object from the perspective of these opposing three sides and then represent any "unseen" features with dotted lines on your drawing. In other words, if there were a round hole in the opposite side of the object, which does not go entirely through the object (unseen feature), then you would represent the hole by drawing a circle using dotted lines on your drawing. In order to represent the depth of the hole you would need to draw dotted lines of a specific length on the drawing that is 90 degrees from the side that has the hole. Essentially, you train yourself to "see through" or visualize the opposite side or hidden side of an object. It is an excellent exercise for your brain and when mastered it can be an extremely helpful tool.

As a practical application of how this "3D space visualization" can help you solve problems or be creative while at home, close your eyes and, from your memory of a real world space, walk through a virtual reality of that space just as you would in the real world. Take in everything as you go, just like you would in viewing a Google map on your computer and then visualize potential problems or possible desired changes or solutions relative to what you see in your mind's eye. After returning to the real world make comparisons to determine if the visualized problems actually existed or if your desired changes or solutions violated any natural laws or physical dimensional constraints i.e. two or more objects occupying the same space or a portion of the same space. This was especially helpful to me in creating new vehicle floor plans. If you use this technique repeatedly you will find that your virtual tour will be enhanced each time with your ever-improving memory of details from your prior comparisons to the real world conditions. If you find this to be less than crystal clear, then please remember that I said, "I don't purport to know how to teach someone how to think outside the box" (I gave it a shot).

CHOOSING THE RIGHT BUSINESS CAREER PATH

Just like me, you will probably be presented with a number of different career paths; so, how do you choose the right one? Since you will most likely be working for an average of 40 years, the answer to this question is critical. How I chose my career path may be of some help.

First, why did I choose business and not engineering after receiving two engineering degrees?

Well, I would like to think I chose a business career over engineering because I didn't feel like I fit in with the engineering types, but the truth is actually much more basic; I lacked a certain something, genius. Being extremely pragmatic I realized that a career in engineering would place me squarely in the middle of the pack; there were simply too many engineering students superior to me intellectually. The difference between their A's and my B's was like the difference between college and high school, no question about it. I did however feel that my early successful experience in my own business at age 16, along with my organizational skills, dedication to hard work and an ability to work well with a diversified group of people, would bode well in a business environment.

The thought of becoming a benevolent dictator in the business world was very appealing as well. Over the course of my career I am sure that many would question my benevolence, but being a dictator was exhilarating; a real sense of being in charge and calling the shots while at the same time carefully masking it as a democracy (not to be tried at home with your spouse). This is the natural order of things in business, but quite another thing in a democratic republic where strict checks and balances are key to a free society (obviously a career in politics was not for me).

Next, why did I pass up a great opportunity to work for a top rated company like P&G to work for a 5 year old relatively unknown company by the name of The Leisure Group?

Having been bitten by the entrepreneurial bug early in life, I was passionate about becoming a top-level executive and eventually becoming the president of a company. My objective was to become a president within 10 to 15 years. Which company would give me the best opportunity to realize my dream? Well, becoming the president of P&G may have taken me 25 years, if at all. Which company would afford me the best possibility of becoming passionate about its products? Well, backpacks, shotguns and bows & arrows were infinitely more exciting to me than toothpaste, soap and toilet paper. Lastly, did I want to be a small fish in a big pond or a big fish in a small pond? The company's wealth and job security were not an issue for me at this stage in my career; The Leisure Group was my clear choice. If your top priority is job security, then you may want to consider a government job, which I consider to be at the opposite end of the spectrum when compared to becoming a capitalist. Your ultimate choice will depend on many factors not the least of which being your acceptable level of risk taking.

After graduate school my business career path resulted in becoming a vice president within 3 years and a president within 10 years. Even though my career path involved taking a number of large risks, it opened up a multitude of great opportunities, both as an employee and as a business owner.

HOW WE SEE THE PROBLEM SOMETIMES IS THE PROBLEM

Just as a person's perception is his or her reality, everyone may have a different perception of a problem, so don't assume anything and ask a lot of questions of the right people before trying to solve a complex problem. To solve any problem we must first start by defining the problem and get a clear consensus of that definition, because sometimes how we see the problem is the problem.

A well-known story is the one about the scientist who was studying frogs in his lab. He commanded a frog to jump and the frog jumped, so he noted in his journal that the frog had jumped upon his command. Next he cut off one of the frog's legs and gave the same command at which the frog jumped, so he noted in his journal that after cutting off one leg and commanding the frog to jump, the frog jumped. He then cut off a second leg and repeated the command and the frog jumped, so he noted in his journal that after cutting off the second leg and commanding the frog to jump, he jumped. He experienced the same exact response after amputating the third leg, which he noted in his journal. But when he amputated the fourth leg and commanded the frog to jump, the frog just sat there; so, he noted in his journal that after amputating all four of the frog's legs, he inexplicably became deaf!

TIME MANAGEMENT

Despite operating a business for 20 hours per week while attending college, I graduated with an engineering degree in four years, but I didn't appreciate it as a lesson learned at the time because I was way too busy to think about it. My schedule forced me to be extremely time conscious, organized and efficient with everything I did. This lesson of necessity has stayed with me and has served me extremely well in the competitive work place over the course of my career. As an example of time management, how much more competitive would you be if you had an extra 3 weeks per year advantage over your competition? Well, if you consider that by taking a ½ hour lunch break instead of an hour, you add 3 weeks of working time to your year (1/2hr per day = 2-1/2hrs per week = 10hrs per month, or 120hrs per year = 3 weeks per year, and this is based on just a 48 week year)!

As Vice President of Operations and CFO of Krystal Enterprises, the world's largest manufacturer of stretched limousines, I helped grow the company by over 350% in the first 4 years of my 15-year tenure. This was greatly helped by not only applying this lunchtime management strategy, but also by the addition of another two weeks per year by foregoing my vacation time. I don't recommend this for everyone, as vacations serve an important function; however, it was highly beneficial. All of the motivating elements were there. Ed Grech, the founder, owner, and president, was the most generous of all of my employers as he embraced the idea that the more he paid me the more money he would make, so it was a win-win situation. Additionally, I found that if I never fell behind in my duties I could handle surprise problems with much less stress, and if you know anything about stress, it is not conducive to effective problem solving.

Fortunately, both my wife of 37 years and I share the same philosophy regarding vacations. We both enjoy our daily home life much more than being at a luxury resort as we are never separated from our dogs and we don't have to go through the hassle of packing and unpacking, not to mention the arduous task of being processed through airport security. Even in retirement, with plenty of time to do whatever we want, we have elected to simply enjoy our home life that we share with both family and friends as often as possible. It is truly the most stress free and enjoyable lifestyle possible. After all, happiness is just a state of mind, which only you can control.

HOW TO SUCCEED IN BUSINSS BY REALLY TRYING

A FISTFUL OF DOLLARS AND PEER PRESSURE

One of the most profitable lessons that I learned at Krystal was that **peer pressure really works**, but you must sell it to your employees in a positive manner in order to get them sufficiently motivated to gain their support. It was costing the company a million dollars per year in fraudulent worker's compensation claims and nothing that we did, not even cash incentives for no lost time accidents, made a dent in it. What I realized was that there was peer pressure working against the company; namely, the peer pressure of not "ratting out" fellow employees for ripping off the company. I knew that I needed to overcome this well ingrained attitude. Then one night it occurred to me that 99% of our employees were honest hard working employees; however, even that loyal 99% were not sufficiently motivated to help save the company money. So, what do we do? How can I get them to think of the company's money as their money? Unfortunately, as good as our employees were, if Krystal were to go bankrupt, they would simply go to another job since unemployment at that time was less than 3% in our area. In fact, it was difficult for us to find people to hire.

So what was the key to make them care about the company's losses? Remembering what my father had said about having a vested interest or skin in the game, all of a sudden it hit me. I needed to give our employees money and then take it away from them if we incurred continued loses. Okay, but how could we possibly do this? I needed to come up with a plan and I needed to sell it to our employees. What we did worked like a charm with annual savings approaching a million dollars after just three years. The savings were the result of less claims being filed and the resulting reduction of our insurance mod rate from 1.99 to 0.57 over three years, which from an insurance company's perspective was over a seventy percent risk reduction factor! The mod rate is a measure of lost time accidents that the insurance companies use in determining the insured's premium payments.

I assembled all 800 production line employees and held up $10,000 of cash in $100 bills in my fist and told them that the company had decided to give them $10,000 a month for each and every month going forward. Boy, it was so quiet you could hear, yes, a pin drop. Talk about getting everyone's undivided attention. Basically I convinced them that it was their money and that the only way that their money would be taken from them was if we had a lost time accident, in which case their money would go to the worker's compensation attorneys to fight fraudulent claims; so, if they wanted to keep their money, then they needed to keep the 1% of our employees from ripping them off. The next fun topic was how our employees wanted to divide up their money. After some exciting deliberation, it was decided that rather than a few big winners it would be better to have 100 employees each win $100 at a safety raffle to be held at the end of each month.

After the meeting the feedback was nothing less than amazing. As an example, one employee said that if someone died on the job during the month in his department they would prop him up in a chair at the safety raffle! Sounds like the movie "A Weekend At Bernie's"!

POWER OF PERSUASION

If you want people to believe something you are about to say, then first tell them something that you know they already believe. Get their heads moving up and down and not side to side. This is like priming the pump so to speak.

You must have the ability to put together cogent arguments and to make salient points. This requires that you have a command of the English language (an excellent vocabulary), complete knowledge of the topic at hand, and the ability to be well organized in your thoughts regarding facts and figures. There is no getting around the importance of a great education to give you valuable tools; however, those tools alone will not guarantee you the power of persuasion. The fact that some of the most persuasive people in history have been relatively uneducated con men is not an indictment against the value of a great education, but rather the importance of having a likeable charismatic personality. Don't underestimate the power of a charismatic personality. As stated earlier, most people incorrectly equate likeability with honesty.

Overwhelming your audience with too many facts or figures can be extremely boring and a real turn off. By not telling everything that you know will help guarantee that a number of insightful questions will be asked, affording you the opportunity to engage them by speaking to their specific concerns. Unscripted questions and answers (Q&A) can have a much greater impact than simply barraging them with information.

Avoid using the word "guarantee" as there are usually exceptions to every rule, and if challenged on something, then I have found it helpful to say, "Anything is possible, but it is highly improbable." There are very few absolutes or guarantees in life except for "death and taxes". This brings to mind the following transcript of an actual court case in which an attorney was grilling a doctor on the witness stand:

Attorney: "Can you guarantee me with absolute certainty that the victim was dead at the time that you performed the autopsy?"

Witness: "Well, his brain was sitting on my desk at the time."

Attorney: "Okay, then wouldn't it still be possible that he was alive?"

Witness: "Only if he was an attorney practicing law."

AVOIDING BANKRUPTCY

What do you do if you find yourself in a desperate cash-strapped turnaround situation and headed for bankruptcy?

As the president of such a company, I was desperate to buy valuable time from 300 creditors in order to avoid a very costly bankruptcy and the negative effect the stigma of a chapter 11-bankruptcy filing would have on our customers. Our competitors would certainly make the most of it by placing doubt in our customer's mind about the company's ability to stand behind its product warranty and subsequently lose valuable sales.

A chapter 11-bankruptcy filing is basically a court ordered stay, or legal protection from creditors, which allows a troubled company to reorganize itself without the pressure of creditors trying to liquidate it through an involuntary bankruptcy (chapter 7).

It requires just 3 creditors to throw a company into an involuntary bankruptcy, so I wrote a compelling letter individually addressed to each of its 300 creditors. I basically said that if they forced the company into bankruptcy then they would be lucky to receive 10 cents on the dollar. I went on to say that I had voluntarily reduced my pay to just one dollar per year for the next year effective immediately. I also offered to open the company's books to them at any time as proof of not only my personal salary reduction, but also to show that none of its creditors had received any preferential treatment. Essentially, I told them that everyone was in this together and that no one would receive any payments unless everyone received a payment in proportion to what was owed them. I also promised to give them a written monthly update on the company's situation for as long as it was still in business.

I am proud to say that, without exception, 100% of the company's creditors agreed to waive payments on the old debt, but the biggest surprise was that only one creditor actually asked to audit the company's books and that creditor was one of its smaller suppliers!

Just like dealing with employees during difficult times, everyone appreciates a shared sacrifice provided they trust you to be fair and honest. To ensure everyone's trust, I took the added precaution of offering to open the company's books as a guarantee that there would be absolutely no trust issues. Remember that it only takes 3 non-believers to thrown a company into bankruptcy, so their trust was absolutely critical.

This approach kept the company out of bankruptcy for what proved to be a crucial period of time; but the underlying lesson is the critical importance of having integrity. As I had mentioned earlier, without it you can forget about having a successful business career.

THE ART OF BOUNCING CHECKS

Let me make this perfectly clear, I don't advocate bouncing checks. Unfortunately, it is a fact of life that checks bounce both in business and in our private lives. There are a variety of reasons and even valid excuses, but the bottom line is that you must distinguish between a "bounced check" and a "bad check". As the signatory on a check you have a fiduciary obligation to whomever the check was made payable. If your check bounces and you can't replace it with a good one, or ensure that the original check will clear if resubmitted, it then becomes a bad check and you could be charged with fraud.

If you deposit a check that bounces it could have a negative ripple effect because you may have needed that deposit to cover your own checks. This can be extremely upsetting, especially if you were not given any advance warning that the check you deposited might not clear.

Well, like many struggling companies, I was a newly hired president of one that was having severe cash flow problems. Paying its suppliers was critical in order to continue receiving their goods to keep the company's production line operating and thereby staying in business. The company was actually slightly profitable at the time as it was turning a major corner; but in order to keep it going, the company desperately needed more cash, so much so that it began to bounce checks and it was my signature on those checks! In fact, 25% of the checks to our suppliers were bouncing on the average every day. With 400 suppliers each receiving one check per month, this amounted to 5 out of 20 checks bouncing every business day.

You are probably thinking that I was being extremely reckless, cavalier, or just plain stupid; however, there was a little method to my madness. It was a dire and almost impossible situation; however, I developed a successful strategy to cope with this situation that lasted for six critical months until the company was firmly back on its feet. The strategy that was developed mitigated the impact on any particular supplier by spreading the pain evenly so to speak.

Every morning at exactly 10 am we would call the bank to see which checks were being presented for payment relative to the company's cash balance and the resulting cash shortfall. Due to the excellent relationship with our bank, we were allowed to pick and choose which checks to cover and which ones to bounce. After our selection we would immediately call the accounts receivable clerk of our suppliers to alert them of the bouncing check. The company did this in a very calm and reserved manner so as not to cause any alarm by having one of our accounting clerks call and down play it as a small glitch at the bank which had been corrected; all our suppliers needed to do was to simply redeposit the check and it would clear. This gave the company about four more business days – enough time to ensure that the re-deposited bounced checks would clear: and, without exception, our suppliers were both thankful and impressed that we had called.

The secret of the company's success was in the development of a matrix, not only ensuring that no check would bounce twice, but also that no supplier would have a check bounce more than once every four months. Since we always called to warn them and always made good on the checks, the occasional bounced check never raised a red flag. It worked like a charm; nonetheless, it was very stressful and required us to keep meticulous records. As a cautionary note, I would never have implemented this strategy had I the slightest doubt that the company was not turning a major corner, as this was only designed as a stopgap short-term solution of necessity. As additional personal security, I also knew that had we ever encountered a major business reversal and even shut down, as a worse case scenario, then there would still be sufficient accounts receivables coming in over time to cover all of the outstanding checks. This was my ultimate safety net since the company's accounts receivables were greater than its outstanding checks by a good margin.

Some companies in our situation would have "factored" their accounts receivable, but the cost for us would have been too expensive due to the company's lack of credit worthiness. If you are not familiar with the term "factoring", it is basically the process of selling accounts receivables at a discount. Not only can this be very expensive, but also the company's customers are required to submit their payments to a third party or lock box, both of which has its own stigma attached. As an example, if you were to discount a 30-day accounts receivable by 5%, then the effective annual interest rate for this factoring would be 60% (5% x 12 months)! Not a very good option for a struggling company.

Furthermore, during this turn around period the company was successful in obtaining a limited credit line from a finance company. As a condition of the financing agreement it was absolutely critical to make payments on or before the due dates. However, our second $25,000 payment was quickly approaching yet we had less than $10,000 in the bank. Not wanting to miss the payment and confident that we would be receiving a customer's check in the amount of $50,000 just prior to the finance company's due date, I took a gamble and mailed the check to the finance company.

Unfortunately, the customer's check had been delayed by several days and would not be in the bank by the time the finance company's check hit. As I waited for the sky to fall, our bank manager called me to say that he had some good news and some bad news, "The bad news is that a $25,000 check was presented for payment this morning and the company only has $8,500 in its account." I then asked what could possibly be the good news and he said, "We are returning the check because they neglected to endorse it!" He went on to say that the check would be returned for payment in about four days, which turned out to be just enough time to get it covered. Talk about the luck of the Irish. Yes, my mother's side of the family is the McGovern's!

Yes, luck always seems to play a role in business, should it be the timing of a product launch or simply being at the right place at the right time. I must say that I have had my fair share of luck in my career, if there is such thing as a fair share. A competitor once told me, "If it weren't for bad luck, I wouldn't have any luck at all!" My wife has often reflected on our good fortune by saying, "We are very lucky to have what we have" to which I would always say, "Yes, and the harder I work the luckier we get!"

Sometimes we do cultivate our own luck. It is my belief that if I had not cultivated a personal relationship with the company's banker, then he would not have allowed us to pick and choose which checks to bounce, much less tolerate the company's continuing financial problems. He also could have very easily ignored the lack of an endorsement and simply bounced the $25,000 check. Never underestimate the importance of business relationships, especially with your banker.

YOU MAY NOT KNOW IT, BUT YOU HAVE A POOR MEMORY

Don't trust your memory. No one will last very long in a job if too many things slip through the cracks. I have learned that most people think that they have an excellent memory, mainly because **they simply don't remember what they have forgotten**!

It is very easy to forget things from time to time, and sometimes it can not only be embarrassing, but it could also cost you a promotion or even your job. Don't be that person. Even with what might seem to be minor details, people will label you as unreliable, which inevitably leads to a limited business future because you will be given less and less responsibility -- not a favorable omen to a bright future. Trust me, regardless of how smart you are, or think you are, you will not survive, much less thrive in the business world if you let things slip through the cracks. Therefore, always carry a voice recorder and dictate messages religiously on a daily basis. If you do not have a recorder with you when something comes up, then write it down and never trust your memory as way too many things happen during the course of the day for you to remember absolutely everything.

HOW TO SUCCEED IN BUSINSS BY REALLY TRYING

You must survive before you can thrive in business. Obviously, the busier you become the more difficult it will become to remember absolutely everything. Unlike the extended period of time that it takes to become known as a person of integrity, becoming known as someone who forgets can happen very quickly. If you keep a recorder with you and use it at work and while driving to and from work, then you will find that the next day you will not remember 100% of what you had logged into that voice recorder, provided you logged at least a dozen things. I say at least a dozen things because if you haven't logged at lease a dozen things, then you are not in a very challenging job. As a test, the following morning write down everything that you can remember from the previous day and then play back your recording to hear in your own words what you had forgotten. Make a habit of using a recorder because as you take on more and more responsibilities in your career the harder it will be to remember absolutely everything, especially the smaller but nonetheless important things.

Another major benefit of the recorder is that you will have less stress in your life from not having to be fearful of forgetting something important. Additionally, I have also found that by keeping your recorder by your bedside (your spouse will love this), you will get a better night's sleep because many things will pop into your head as you are placing yourself into the relaxed state of sleep; and, you don't want to be concerned about forgetting something the next morning that may be very important. Once it is on the recorder it will give you peace of mind and you can forget it for a good night's sleep.

"A clear conscience is the sign of a poor memory." Steven Wright

LEAD BY EXAMPLE

When it comes to leadership, always lead by example and never take the approach of "Do as I say, not as I do". Never expect more from your employees than you expect from yourself. This approach will help perpetuate a team spirit and gain you a tremendous amount of respect from those that you lead. This will obviously require hard work and dedication on your part, but I have learned that the benefits will be incredible in terms of attitudes and results. For example, if you require your salaried employees to work over the weekend without extra pay, they will feel a lot better about it if they know that you will be there with them, as opposed to knowing that you are off skiing.

During tough economic times, I learned that, despite hardships, employees appreciate shared sacrifice. Faced with the need to reduce the cost of our office staff by 25%, in lieu of a layoff I cut wages by 20% and reduced hours by 20% (a four day work week). To make up for the 5% cost cutting shortfall, I required that all top management, including myself, to take a 30% pay cut but with no time off work. Yes, this cost us personal income in the short run; but, it worked out in the long run, as no one quit and hence we did not have to hire and train new employees when business eventually picked up.

DON'T PRIORITIZE YOUR SCHEDULE

This may sound counter intuitive, but sometimes employees will make the mistake of actually working on their top priorities first! How stupid is that? This may seem like a crazy statement, so let me explain. I have seen way too many employees set aside a dozen 30 minute projects to work solely on a top priority project that consumes 100% of their time for two or three weeks while the lesser priority projects get totally ignored despite complaints from upset business associates who are depending on their support. Well, the bottom line is that this person is actually being a procrastinator, but doesn't recognize it for what it is because he or she is still working hard on the most important project. In their minds, they are immune to criticism because, after all, they have the perfect excuse as they are working on the company's most important project.

An IT manager developed a pompous attitude towards his associates for their complaints about his lack of support. If this was not bad enough, he then made them pay the price for complaining by placing their needs at the bottom of his list. Inevitably his managerial position was rather short. **The key is not to prioritize your schedule, but rather to schedule your priorities.** If you can't knock out these lower priority items during the course of the day while working on your top priority items, then it is necessary to make time for these items either at lunch or after normal working hours. Never think that you can simply ignore them just because everyone knows that you are busy. **The lesson is that you simply can't afford to let less time consuming lower priority projects stack up on you.**

"It is better to be a little behind than a big behind." Anonymous

MEETINGS

Meetings are critical to ensure that everyone is on the same page relative to business plans. Inevitably there are misunderstandings or miscommunications in any business that more often than not are discovered during group sessions. There is, however, a fine line between too many meetings and too few. Meetings take away from everyone's work and some may view meetings as boring; yet, just one error uncovered could save the company a lot of money by avoiding potential problems. Meetings don't have to be entertaining, just informative and well organized. Therefore, always prepare an agenda and distribute it before a meeting so that everyone has time to prepare.

One of the problems with meetings is that they tend to last too long because some employees are not well organized, or a specific problem is under intense discussion and there is not enough time to complete everything on the agenda. You must be a good time manager; so if a specific topic begins to dominate the meeting, it is best to schedule a sub meeting with a limited number of affected employees at another time and then update everyone at the next regularly scheduled meeting. There should also be an ending time for the meeting that everyone will naturally have a vested interest, like noon to go to lunch, or at quitting time, as everyone will be interested in going home.

There are some employees who will be offended if not asked to attend a meeting while others will say they are too busy to attend. I have learned to limit the meetings to just the department heads on a regular basis and then, on occasion, invite others to discuss specific projects when they are the ones most knowledgeable. I subscribe to just one regularly scheduled two hour meeting on a weekly basis. I have also found that scheduling the meetings on the same day of the week is easier for everyone to remember and allows everyone to plan their schedules around that day for weeks or even months in advance. This helps ensure that everyone will be in attendance with no excuse of a prior scheduling conflict.

There are those who always come late to meetings, so what do you do? Wait for them? Start the meeting without them? Well, I have heard of several radical solutions. For instance, inform everyone in advance that the conference room doors will be locked 5 minutes after the starting time, or simply charge $100 for anyone who enters the room more than 5 minutes after the scheduled meeting time. Holding up a meeting until the offending party shows up works well for subsequent meetings. This is because of peer pressure from those who are upset for being inconvenienced as everyone has better things to do than to just sit and wait. Instead of speeding through the meeting to make up for the delayed start, I have intentionally extended the meeting into the lunch hour and made it clear why, which also helped with the peer pressure for subsequent meetings.

So what do you do with a boss or higher up whom routinely shows up late or not at all? Well, this has actually happened to me on numerous occasions, so I would simply start the meetings on time and fill them in on critical items via e-mail afterwards. I also let them know that I would be willing to hold up future meetings for them if they let me know that they will be running late, otherwise I will hold the meeting as scheduled.

Lastly, I found it helpful to send a weekly e-mail reminder on the morning before each meeting, especially for those who tended to be tardy.

THE RULE OF 72

I was surprised to learn "The Rule of 72" from a fellow executive, who always impressed me with his ability to very quickly and accurately calculate the time it would take to double his money without the use of a calculator or a compound interest table. This is how it works, you simply divide the compound interest rate into 72 to get the number of years it would take to double your money. Conversely, if you divide the number of years that you would like to double your money into 72, you will get the compound interest rate that would be required. If you really want to be creative, you can very easily calculate the quadrupling of your money by simply using this system twice. In other words, find the time to double your money and then double it again in the same amount of time. As an example, if you want to know how long it will take you to double your money at 7.2% interest, then you divide 7.2 into 72 to get 10 years. In an additional 10 years at 7.2% you will double the doubled money for a quadrupling of your money in a total of 20 years. If you want to double your money in 6 years, then you will need a compound interest rate of return of 12% (72 divided by 6). Please keep in mind that this system works very well except at the extremes like doubling in 1 year at a 72% interest rate; but, otherwise, it works for reasonable interest rates or reasonable periods of time.

Okay it is not rocket science, but I have found it very useful on a number of occasions as a quick litmus test for an investment before spending too much time thinking about whether the rate of return is too low.

So what do you think about doubling your money in 12 years? Of course, your answer has to be weighed against the risk factor. A 6% annual return may sound great in a bank account that is FDIC insured, but not in a speculative start up business.

INTERVIEWING APPLICANTS IS A LISTENING PROCESS

As an interviewer never start an interview with questions; rather, engage in casual conversation until the candidate is relaxed and comfortable in your presence. The more relaxed and friendly you appear, the quicker this initial process will take. I have found that it usually takes about 10 or 15 minutes to completely break the ice and gain their confidence; but, regardless of how long it takes don't rush it. Once this is accomplished, I have learned that most candidates will tell you a lot more about themselves than you could possibly ask. Still, this process will require you to ask some probing questions, like what do they consider to be their strongest asset, which usually gets a long well prepared response. Next I ask them what they think are their weakest points and ask for examples of how it worked against them in the past. No two interviews are the same; so, let them do most of the talking. Surprisingly enough, most candidates will trap themselves in a conversation that they never intended on discussing. No matter what they say, go with the flow; the more that you appear to support their point of view, the more they will reveal about their past employment problems.

Once I interviewed a guy for a purchasing manager position in which I asked him if he had ever had a problem with an employee. He emotionally responded that he was given a task of training an employee for the purchasing department and when she subsequently failed, she blamed his training. This led to an ugly confrontation whereupon he was issued a written warning, which he said he did not deserve. He got so upset relaying this story to me that I seriously questioned his emotional stability. Up until that point, the interview was going just fine.

I learned a valuable lesson early in my career while I was an operations manager for a manufacturing company. The company had a need for an accounting assistant, which in retrospect should have been an easy position to fill; however, I unwittingly decided to make a career of it. Usually it requires about a half dozen interviews, or less, finding at least one qualified candidate; it was not until my twenty-first interview that I found an acceptable candidate. My boss at the time and good friend, Ken Rentzsch, will never let me forget this seemingly endless process; he has ribbed me about it from time to time over the course of the past 40 years. Since the position required the use of an adding machine, I wanted the candidates to have a sense for the magnitude of the numbers that they would be dealing with and be able to recognize an error in terms of the decimal point being off by a multiple of 10. In other words, if a certain cost item for a month was historically about $10,000, then I wanted them to have the capacity to raise a mental flag if their calculator showed $100,000, a ten-fold error due to the slip of a decimal point. In other words, I wanted someone who could think.

Consequently, I designed what I thought was a simple test; however, what I learned was that not only do applicants not expect a math test on an interview, but their I.Q. drops to below room temperature due to the stress! Since all of the applicants were young women with high school diplomas, I designed a word problem, which I thought they could easily relate; namely, "If you could purchase 10 **hair curlers** for $5, then what would the cost be of just one?" I offered them a pen and paper, I allowed an unlimited amount of time and I even left the room to help them concentrate. Well, I received answers ranging from $2 to $8 with one applicant refusing to even attempt a guess! Not until my twenty-first applicant, Katy Karman, the daughter of the famed Los Angeles Times publisher, Otis Chandler, did I find a winner, and she turned out be an excellent employee with a great personality to boot!

Being single at the time, some of my office associates were wondering if I was speed dating! Ken knew that I was simply trying to fill the position with the best possible candidate, but it became evident that he thought I was being very cruel at the time when he referred to my applicants as "Those poor girls!" Never since have I placed an applicant in such a stressful position; so, I really did learn a lesson, but who knew?

"Since light travels faster than sound, some people appear bright, until you hear them speak." Brian Williams

HOW DO YOU KNOW THAT YOU ARE HIRING THE RIGHT PERSON?

Like most decisions in business, hiring is a judgment call and only the test of time will determine if the person you have chosen is the right person for the job.

Everything being equal relative to the interview and background checks, you must still ultimately rely on your gut feeling as to the candidate whom you feel would best fit into your organization. To extend the potential of your gut feeling, I have found that it is often helpful to walk a candidate to his or her vehicle. This affords you the opportunity to inspect their vehicle, not from the perspective of judging the model year and make, but from the perspective of how well the vehicle is maintained. For example, was the exterior reasonably clean? Was the interior clean as opposed to seeing paper cups and hamburger wrappers lying around? Yes, how we dress or our appearance is not the only visual clue to evaluating someone, but seeing how well we care for our property, like our vehicle, is another.

Over the course of my career I have been extremely fortunate to have over a 95% success rate with my new hires. Unfortunately, however, not everyone will be the right person for the job as was the case in my experience with Lisa. The company was in need of an accounts payable clerk and after interviewing half-dozen candidates we locked in on Lisa as our clear favorite. She not only had 5 years of experience, but also was very personable and deemed to be an excellent fit with our other employees. The Human Resources (HR) Manager performed a favorable background check, so we hired her. Lisa had requested that we not contact her current employer until after we had hired her, which was normal and proper protocol. The company's protocol was for the HR Manager to perform a verification of employment with her last employer immediately after she began working for us. Unfortunately, our HR Manager told me that Lisa's prior employer would only give out the dates that she had worked there and no additional information. This was not that uncommon for companies to take this position regarding past employees due to the risk of being sued for liable if their response was less than favorable resulting in the applicant losing out on an employment opportunity.

Due to the sensitive nature of this accounting position, I wanted more information; so, I called Lisa's last employer's HR Manager, Susan, to see if there was any past employment problems. Susan was very courteous but she gave me no additional information by citing company policy and there was absolutely no hint of past employment problems. The conversation could have ended there; but, in the absence of any voluntary favorable comments, I asked one last probing question, "Is Lisa eligible for rehire?" After she said "no" she absolutely refused to give any explanation as to why. Not being one to give up easily, I got her to agree to give me more information provided I could obtain a "hold harmless" letter signed by Lisa. Essentially, I drafted a letter that stated that Lisa would not sue them for sharing her past employment details with me. I presented the letter for Lisa to sign and informed her that if she refused, then I would have no other recourse but to terminate her employment. She agreed and signed it.

California is an "at will" state which means that an employer can terminate an employee at its will for any reason that is not illegal, like discriminating against someone for their race, creed, religion, age, weight, handicap or gender.

After receiving my letter, Susan called to inform me that Lisa had been fired for inappropriate behavior. There had been a breach of trust as she had allowed her boy friend to steal a blank company check, which he subsequently forged and cashed. The company had successfully prosecuted him but decided to simply fire her; hence, nothing had shown up on her criminal background check.

It was sad because Lisa was working out very well and everyone loved her, but I had no choice other than to fire her for lying on her application regarding her past employment.

Several of my other hires didn't work out for different reasons as well. The most common scam was to tell us that they were currently working when they had actually been fired. I guess they were either hoping we wouldn't follow up to verify their past employment, or they were hoping that their initial job performance would overshadow their lie if and when it was exposed.

To help from getting scammed in this way, which wasted both valuable time and resources, I developed a plan that was both caring and foolproof.

Whenever I hired someone who said that they were working and needed to give their two weeks notice, I would call them at work during their second week's notice to see how their resignation had been received, confirmed their arrival for the following week and let them know that we were really looking forward to working with them. Without exception, all of my newly hired applicants were very pleased that I had called, as switching jobs can be very stressful. However, on one occasion when I had called and asked the receptionist to speak to Bob Olsen, she said that no one by that name worked there. Since Bob had told me that he reported directly to the president, I asked to speak to him. Well, the president of the company told me that Bob had actually worked for him several years earlier but that he had been let go after about a year due to being incompetent in his field of work. He also said that he believed that Bob had been unemployed ever since, as he had been collecting unemployment benefits.

With that revelation, I immediately called one of my other applicants whom I had previously interviewed and quickly filled that position. Oh, when Bob showed up the following Monday for his anticipated first day of work he was more than a little surprised that his scam had been uncovered.

The lesson here is that lying to a potential employer is never a good idea. Since there are two sides to every story, if you are ever fired or let go for any reason, then simply tell the truth and give your side of the story to mitigate the negative stigma. Unless the reason was for theft, I believe your chances are pretty good that your honesty will be rewarded with an opportunity to prove yourself. Most fair-minded people believe in giving second chances.

DON'T HIRE MARRIED COUPLES

I have never hired married couples to work in the same department or even in the same company; however, I have worked for several companies that had employed both. Generally speaking, those that worked in separate departments were usually not a problem, but for those working in the same department it was very problematic for both the couple and the company. The reasons should be obvious but I will give you an example of a worst-case scenario.

I was a vice president of a company that owned a financing subsidiary, which employed David, the President, and his wife, Kathy, who was his Credit Analyst. They actually got married after the company had hired them and it became a huge problem.

After having been married for about a year, Kathy called the police to their home and had David arrested for kicking her in the leg during a domestic squabble. David told us that he had gotten really upset and had kicked at their boat, but she had walked by and he had accidently kicked her. As the President of our subsidiary company, the company bailed him out; however, Kathy subsequently obtained a restraining order against him requiring that he come no closer than 200 feet from her. They may or may not have been able to work in the same office together; however, the office was not large enough for them to be separated by 200 feet.

Other than this problem, both were excellent employees. As a temporary solution, we relocated David to one of the company's manufacturing facilities located about a mile away. This proved to be extremely inefficient for him to manage his office staff of 10 employees. It would have worked better had we relocated her, but we were concerned that it may be viewed as a retaliatory action against her with the possibility of her filing a discrimination lawsuit against the company.

The president of the parent company had the perfect solution. He arranged for another finance company to hire her away from us. Talk about the Wisdom of Solomon! They were thrilled to be able to hire her and we resolved an untenable situation. This is not only an example of a win/win solution but also of thinking outside the box.

As a follow up to this story, David and Kathy reunited after about a six-month separation and by all accounts they appeared to have resolved their personal differences.

A married couple working together is not a good idea. The lessons learned is not only to not hire married couples, but also to make it a written company policy in the employee manual that if employees were to marry each other, then one of them would be required to resign as a condition of continued employment of the other.

YOU MUST KNOW YOUR NUMBERS TO FORECAST

In simple terms, accounting only involves a basic knowledge of arithmetic: addition, subtraction, division and multiplication. The trick to understanding accounting is to know when to do what. Of all of my classes, I loved accounting best because it simply made way too much sense. I found it to be intuitive, and infinitely less complicated than calculus or advanced engineering mathematics, which I had taken before my first accounting class.

Early in my career I learned that a good understanding of accounting was absolutely critical with respect to my perception of how I viewed companies in which I either operated or invested. It was by accident while working with numbers 30 years ago that I learned to combine my knowledge of accounting with algebra, and that's when I truly felt empowered. This knowledge also allowed me to generate information first hand and draw my own conclusions without any filtering through an accountant.

Essentially, I learned that it was relatively easy to develop an algebraic formula, or model, which would not only allow me to calculate a company's Break Even Point (BEPT) but it also allowed me to make a variety of Profit & Loss (P&L) projections based on a number of different assumptions.

I learned to visualize a company's cost structure in terms of its components of variable and fixed overhead costs. Then it was simply a matter of creating a formula using the relationship between all of the costs and sales to solve a zero sum algebraic formula. In other words, at what level of sales revenue does the profit or loss equal exactly zero, which is by definition the BEPT? This analysis does require a certain number of assumptions, which if found to be wrong could radically change the outcome, but it is still simple algebra with just one equation and one unknown. It is not as difficult as it may sound so bear with me.

The P&L formula is simply **(Sales Revenue) – (Costs) = P&L**, **which is equal to zero at the BEPT**.

The following is a simplified example of this type of analysis. If you thought that the answer was $8 to the **hair curler test** in <u>Interviewing Applicants Is A Listening Process</u>, then it would be best to skip this section.

Let's say that you are in the transportation business and you drive your customers from their home to the airport for an average of 50 miles total per trip and with sales revenues and a cost structure as follows:

Sales Revenue	$100 per trip
Cost of Driver	40 per trip (Variable expense)
Cost of Fuel	10 per trip (Variable expense)
Vehicle Deprec.	10 per trip (Variable expense)
Maint., Ins. & Misc.	5 per trip (Variable expense)
Facility Rent	5,000 per month (Fixed expense)
Staff Salaries	30,000 per month (Fixed expense)

Using our P&L formula to find the BEPT:
(Sales Revenue) – (Costs) = P&L
(Price/trip)(Trips/month) – (Var. costs) – (Fixed costs) = P&L
Let X = number of trips per month
The Price is $100/trip
The total Variable cost is $65/trip
The total Fixed cost is $35,000/month
Now solving for X **when the P&L is zero**:
100(X) - 65(X) – 35,000 = 0
 35(X) – 35,000 = 0
 X = **1,000 trips per month**

So, at 1,000 trips or $100,000 (1,000 trips x $100) of sales revenue per month we break even.

Please note that the **"Profit Margin"** is the sales revenue less the variable overhead costs, which in our example is $35 or 35% of the sales revenue (100 – 65 = 35). I look at this **"Profit Margin"** as the **Contribution of each sale towards covering the fixed overhead costs and profit**. **In other words, once the fixed overhead is covered then we are at our BEPT and each additional sale (trip) will generate a profit of $35**.

So how many vehicles would we need to operate at the BEPT? Can you answer that question? Do you even have enough information to answer that question? Okay, now is the time that you must put on your pragmatic thinking cap and make a few assumptions. You will not always be given all of the information on a silver platter. In the world of business you will always be required to make judgment calls or educated guesses. Those who master the art of doing this will be the ones who will become the most successful.

Since we know that each trip requires an average of 50 miles, then at a BEPT of 1,000 trips per month we would have a grand total of 50,000 miles (50 x 1,000) per month. If we assume that an average vehicle will be driven **5,000 miles per month**, then we would need **10 vehicles. Each vehicle will be operating at the rate of 100 trips per 4-week month (50 x 100 = 5,000 miles),** or 25 trips per week, or 5 trips per day based on a 5-day workweek. Therefore, each vehicle would be driven **250 miles per day**, or 5,000 miles per four-week month (20 days). At this rate the vehicles would log 60,000 miles per year for a useful life of 240,000 miles or four years, which is reasonable. Does driving **250 miles** per day per vehicle sound possible or reasonable? If we assume that each vehicle will average 25 miles per hour, which includes the time for pick-up and delivery (2 hours per trip), then a 10-hour workday would be required to log 250 miles (250/25), which is very reasonable. So, how much will our drivers earn per hour during their 10 hour day? As you will remember, the driver receives $40 per trip as part of the variable overhead costs and at 5 trips per day they would earn $200 per day or $20 per hour for a 10-hour day (plus tips), which is a fair wage for this type of work (not too physically demanding and not highly skilled). Consequently, we should not have a problem recruiting good drivers.

Also, at a purchase price of $48,000 per vehicle, we would have a capital expenditure requirement of $480,000 ($48,000 x 10) for starters. Please note that in order to generate a profit we would need to book more than 1,000 trips per month and this would require the acquisition of additional vehicles. Starting with the eleventh vehicle we would generate a profit of $35 for each $100 trip, and if we could generate the maximum number of 100 trips per month per vehicle, then the company would generate a profit of $3,500 per month per additional vehicle. This will be true for each additional vehicle as long as the fixed overhead costs are not increased, which at some point may be required to support the higher level of activity. These additional vehicles, which will be operating above our BEPT, will only be subject to variable overhead expenses, as all of the fixed overhead expenses will have already been covered by the first 10 vehicles.

Since breaking-even is no fun, lets see how much we can make if we were able to book **1,500 trips** per month. The additional 500 trips would require the acquisition of 5 more vehicles at a cost of $240,000 ($48,000 x 5) with each vehicle operating at 100 trips per month.

Keep in mind that **100(X) – 65(X) – 35,000 = Profit & Loss and is equal to zero only at the BEPT**; so, it is simply a matter of plugging in the number of trips as follows:

100(1,500) – 65(1,500) = $52,500 **Profit Margin**
Less fixed O.H. (35,000)
Profit **$17,500 per month**

(Since we know that each trip above 1,000 trips per month will generate a profit of $35, a shortcut calculation would simply be 500 trips x $35 = $17,500 profit per month.)

On the other hand, what if we could only generate 800 trips or $80,000 of sales revenue per month, then how much would we lose? Well, the analysis would go like this:

100(800) – 65(800) = $28,000 **Profit Margin**
Less fixed O.H. (35,000)
Loss **($7,000) per month**

(The shortcut calculation would simply be the number of trips below our BEPT of 1,000 trips per month times $35, or 200 trips x $35 = $7,000 loss per month.)

The variable depreciation expense of $10 per trip was calculated based on a $48,000 vehicle purchase price. Dividing $48,000 by a useful life of four years gives us a depreciation expense of $12,000 per year or $1,000 per month. At 100 trips per vehicle per month our expense per trip would be $10 ($1,000/100 = $10). At the end of the four-year useful life for each vehicle it will need to be replaced, so where do we get the money to replace those vehicles? Well, as you will remember, depreciation expense is not a cash flow item so the $10 depreciation expense per trip must be placed in a savings account to cover its replacement cost. In four years you will have saved $48,000 for every vehicle that requires replacement (4,800 trips x $10 = $48,000).

The variable fuel expense was based on a 50-mile trip at 20 mpg and a fuel price of $4 per gallon, which would require 2-1/2 gallons (50/20 = 2-1/2) at an expense of $10 per trip (2-1/2 x $4 = $10). Keep in mind that if fuel prices drops to $3 per gallon, then the expense would then be $7.50 per trip (2-1/2 gal x $3 = $7.50).

Excited yet?

Forecasting is always based on a number of assumptions, so as an example, you can calculate how a change in your pricing structure would affect the bottom line. Keep in mind that our P&L model is simply represented by **100(X) - 65(X) – 35,000 = P&L**. If you had to drop your price from $100 to **$70 per trip**, due to competition to maintain **1,000 trips per month**, then your loss would be as follows with **X = 1,000 trips:**

$$\underline{70}(X) - 65(X) = 5,000 \textbf{ Profit Margin}$$
Less fixed O.H. (35,000)
Loss   (30,000) per month

As you can see that this type of an analysis is a crucial component in determining your pricing for either products or services; therefore, we will be returning to this airport transportation example shortly when we discuss <u>Price Sensitivity</u> and <u>Pricing Your Products Or Services</u>.

"Forecasting is difficult, especially if it is about the future."
Sam Goldwyn

Michael Hill

EFFECTIVE REPORT WRITING

Unlike my long-winded explanation of forecasting, effective report writing is just the opposite. In other words, would you want to reread my analysis a second time assuming that you actually read it the first time? The bottom line is the bottom line; so, just cut to the chase and spare your boss the task of understanding how you got there. If your boss questions your process, then you will be prepared. It is always best to get to the bottom line as quickly as possible but it will always be of the utmost importance to state all of your assumptions. Your boss will be more interested in questioning your assumptions than your ability to perform a mathematical equation, as the assumptions are absolutely critical to the bottom line. Stating your assumptions will also protect you if your forecast is found to be wrong; and, probably 99% of all forecasts will be inaccurate in one form or another principally because all of your assumptions would have to be correct in order for the forecast to be accurate. As an example, if the sales-department ends up discounting your products or services by an average of 10%, then your bottom line numbers will obviously be wrong but at least your forecast will not have been wrong provided you included a sales assumption of not discounting.

I actually learned this lesson the hard way while working at The Leisure Group. I was given the task of calculating the optimal number of bullets to inventory for each size bullet at its Sierra Bullets plant, which manufactured bullets (projectiles only) for the reloading market. The objective was to optimize the inventory level of each bullet relative to its sales volume, carrying cost and the cost of changing over the production tooling dies. The optimal inventory level would minimize the probability of running out of stock of any particular bullet. It would also minimize the overall cost of producing and inventorying all of the bullets, which would be produced by a limited number of machines. With 35 different sizes, shapes or caliber bullets, I used a recursive formula that accounted for everything from the cost of both carrying inventory and changing over the tooling dies to the limited number of production machines available to produce the bullets. I gained this knowledge from my educational training in the field of **Operations Research**, which by definition is the optimal allocation of limited resources through the use of statistical analysis and probability theory.

Each bullet required about three pages of calculations; so, I submitted approximately 100 pages with an answer for each bullet at the end of every third page. I incorrectly assumed that my boss would like to see the work that I had performed. As this was my first job out of graduate school, I was really excited to see what my boss, Reid Calcot, thought of my work. Since my annual review was just two weeks after I had submitted my report, I would know soon enough. Well, Reid's words were absolutely priceless, "Are you shitting me, or is this for real?" I convinced him that it was for real; so, he gave me a big raise and assigned me to my next project of moving a company from California to Arkansas.

Instead of requiring my boss to read through 100 pages to get the answer for each of the 35 bullets, I should have simply summarized my answers on a single page and not bored him with the other 99 pages. If he were to question my work, then at that point I would have been well prepared to bore him.

You may find it interesting to note that the science of **Operations Research** was actually developed during World War II as a means of patrolling the Atlantic Ocean in search of German submarines (U-boats). Basically, a grid was developed of the optimal flight patterns to maximize the probability of searching the ocean at any given time with a limited number of airplanes.

"If you can't dazzle them with brilliance, then baffle them with bullshit." W.C. Fields

PRICE SENSITIVITY

Price sensitivity is basically the magnitude of the effect of a small price change, whether it is an increase or a decrease, on the sales volume. If the effect of a small price change on the sales volume is significant, then your products or services are considered to be price sensitive. On the other hand, if the effect of a small price change on the sales volume were very little then your product or services would not be considered to be very price sensitive.

Knowing the profit margins for your products or services is critical to managing your business; without it, you would be flying blind.

In the airport transportation example from You Must Know Your Numbers To Forecast we had a total variable overhead cost of $65 per trip; therefore, once the total fixed overhead cost of $35,000 was covered, the company would generate a profit of $35 for every $100 trip. At $100 per trip we learned that the break-even point was 1,000 trips per month. If your sales manager tells you that the company could increase the number of trips by 20% with a 10% price reduction would it be a good decision? Can you answer that question?

Unless your products or services are highly price sensitive, it would be doubtful that a 10% price reduction ($100 to $90) would actually result in a 20% increase in the number of trips (1,000 to 1,200). Keep in mind that **your sales personnel are not responsible for the company's profits, but rather the volume of sales from which they derive their commissions. This is a built-in conflict of interest** and must be watched very carefully. I can't count the number of times that I have been challenged by the sales department to make a potentially bad decision. You don't want to demoralize your sales personnel despite being skeptical of their claim of a 20% increase in the number of trips with a 10% price reduction; so, first take an analytical approach to see if their proposal makes any sense from a bottom line standpoint. If it passes that test, then the price sensitivity issue can be addressed.

Since the 10% price reduction or $10 ($100 to $90) comes right off the bottom line, your profit margin in our example would be reduced from $35 to $25 per trip. **As you can see, a 10% price reduction results in approximately a 30% profit margin reduction**. This reduction in profit margin will effectively increase your break-even point (BEPT) from 1,000 to 1,400 trips per month, which is calculated as follows: $90(X) - 65(X) - 35,000 = 0 =$ BEPT; therefore, $X = 1,400$ <u>where X is the number of trips to break even</u>. You will recall previously that the BEPT was 1,000 trips per month based on $100 per trip.

A 10% price reduction would require a 40% increase in trips (1,000 to 1,400) just to break even, so even if a 20% increase to 1,200 trips were possible it would still fall short of maintaining your BEPT. Additionally, you would only be generating a profit of $25 instead of $35 for every trip above the BEPT.

There is also a capital investment consideration. You will remember that 10 vehicles at $48,000 each were required to support 1,000 trips per month; so 1,400 trips would require 40% more vehicles, or an additional 4 vehicles at a cost of $192,000. Even at the proposed 20% increase to 1,200 trips, it would require 2 additional vehicles at a cost of $96,000.

Obviously their proposal will not fly but <u>your analysis will arm you with the reason for its rejection without even having to address the price sensitivity issue</u>, which could be a very contentious discussion.

CONFLICTS OF INTEREST WITHIN YOUR COMPANY

It is extremely important to expand upon my comment in the prior section regarding the conflict of interest between the company's profits and the sales department's commissions. Basically, sales people make their living selling their ideas, products or services, so they can be extremely persuasive especially when they are passionate about their belief in increasing sales and their resulting sales commissions.

As a CFO (Chief Financial Officer) I have had the unenviable position of being the spoiler of many a sales proposal based on my analysis of the bottom line. Since most sales personnel are persuasive and have very fragile egos or sensitive pocket books, I have found it necessary to handle them very carefully by investing the time to explain my analysis in detail.

Fortunately, I have always been able to debunk unreasonable claims analytically without having to debate or attack their beliefs regarding price sensitivity which would be a much more difficult task. Just imagine how difficult it would be to tell your sales personnel that they don't know what they are talking about!

From a conflict of interest standpoint, had the proposal in my example been implemented it would have resulted in the company either losing money or making less profit, not to mention the need to purchase additional vehicles. On the other hand, the sales personnel would most likely have benefited from higher commissions based on increased sales, even if the increase was less than their projection, as a 10% price reduction might result in some incremental increase in sales.

As mentioned earlier, if someone doesn't have skin in the game, they don't share your interests; however, be careful not to alienate yourself from the sales personnel as sales revenue will always be the lifeblood of any company.

PRICING YOUR PRODUCTS OR SERVICES

Pricing your products or services can be extremely difficult but there will always be a number of basics that must be considered.

Since sales revenues drive your company, you must position your prices for products or services to ensure that you will be successful. Being successful means that you will not only generate sales but also generate an acceptable profit. A marketing analysis can be extremely complex involving everything from product placement to price sensitivity and everything in-between.

From a financial analysis standpoint, your pricing must tie into the volume of sales and its resulting profit or loss. Having been involved in a number of turnaround companies, this analysis is never a simple task. As president of one of these companies, my well-meaning executive secretary, Joan, recommended that I simply price each product at a profit. Why hadn't I thought of that? If only it were that simple!

Joan was so sincere and genuinely wanting to help that I felt compelled to explain the dilemma; namely, how would the fixed overhead costs be allocated in our pricing? Variable overhead costs are easy to allocate as these costs are directly related to each product or service. On the other hand, the fixed overhead costs are not so easy to allocate, as we would need to know exactly how much product or services will be sold.

In the prior transportation example, if we assume that we will be making only 100 trips to the airport each month, then the $35,000 fixed overhead would have to be borne by the revenue generated by just 100 trips instead of 1,000 trips in order to break even. Instead of charging $100 per trip, we would be required to charge **$415 per trip** ($35,000 / 100 trips = $350, plus the variable overhead costs per trip of $65) just to break even!

In order to keep our competitive rate at $100 per trip and still break even at 100 trips per month we would have to reduce our fixed overhead cost from $35,000 to $3,500 per month ($3,500/ 100 trips = $35, plus the variable overhead cost per trip of $65 gives us a total of $100). Obviously we would have our work cut out for us in reducing the fixed overhead in order to take advantage of a "smaller economy of scale". Since we would only be required to operate one vehicle in order to log 100 trips per month, a possible solution would be to operate from our house and eliminate 90% of our staff. This would allow us to survive, however, in order to be profitable we would need to be able to do one of three things; reduce our fixed overhead costs even further, increase our price per trip, or increase the number of trips per month, which would require the purchase of one or more additional vehicles and may require an increase in our advertising budget.

As you can see, a company's bottom line is a numbers game. It is the volume of sales of your business that will dictate both your pricing structure and your economy of scale.

"We are losing money on every sale but making up for it with volume." Anonymous

ECONOMY OF SCALE

"Economy of scale" is basically the size of your operations with its associated fixed overhead costs and its potential for producing products or services relative to the market place demands and your ability to generate a profit. The size of your operations is dictated by your projected sales volume, working capital and level of acceptable risk taking.

The advantage of a larger economy of scale relative to your competitors may be that your operations allow you to take advantage of bull markets (strong markets) while your competitors are constrained by a limited production capacity.

On the other hand, during bear markets (weak markets) your smaller competitors may have the advantage of a smaller economy of scale with their lower fixed overhead and lower breakeven point. Consequently, while you are operating at say 50% of capacity and losing money your competitor may be better positioned to weather the bad times and even make a profit with their lower overhead costs while operating at or near full capacity.

There is a lot to be said about keeping your company small or "lean and mean". I have seen many companies expand their operations during the good times only to regret it during the bad times. As mentioned earlier, **the bad times will always come, as it is just a matter of time.**

Growing your company can be very expensive in terms of both capital expenditures and increased fixed overhead costs. The benefits of a larger economy of scale are usually two fold: you will have a greater production capacity to meet a higher sales demand and enjoy an increase in production efficiencies; both of which will maximize your profits. The production cost per unit produced usually decreases with an increase in scale as fixed costs are spread over a higher number of units produced. Also efficiencies are usually greater as well with an increase in scale due to lower variable costs like direct labor and raw material costs with the purchasing power that comes from a greater number of parts being purchased.

It has been my experience that the transition to larger economies of scale is a natural evolutionary process in any growing company. When the sales demand increases for a company's products there is naturally more and more pressure placed on production to produce more product.

Increasing production quickly was one of my specialties, which utilized the concept of "division of labor". This concept dates back to Adam Smith (The Wealth of Nations), but I took my inspiration from Henry Ford who used this concept with great success in the assembly line production of automobiles.

Division of labor is a very intuitive concept and I like to equate it to the basic concept of digging a hole. For example, if one man can dig a hole in 8 hours (8 man-hours), then two men can dig it in 4 hours (8 man-hours). Taking this analogy to its logical conclusion, if we hired 8 men then they could dig the hole in one hour (8 man-hours), right? Well, the problem with this analogy is that at some point we will reach a point of diminishing returns. In other words, we will not only fail to achieve any improved efficiencies with each man performing the same function, but we will see a decrease due to the hole being too small to adequately accommodate more than say 4 men. Each additional man will actually reduce efficiencies as they begin getting into each other's way. Thus it may take 8 men an entire day to dig the hole.

The solution to this problem in a manufacturing environment is to stretch out the production line, thereby creating additional workstations. This will require more space or a larger economy of scale. The increased scale will not only provide more space for the workers, but the operations can then increase efficiencies by specializing the labor force, or by dividing the labor force (division of labor) into simpler functions that are less time consuming. This will not only allow for an increase in overall production but each worker will become more efficient while performing less functions. The workers will become masters of their trade, even if it is simply installing lug nuts on just the left rear wheel of every car on the assembly line. Despite an increase in production, a decrease in the number of functions being performed will usually results in an increase in quality.

I have found that the best mindset for expanding your business is to have an eye on what you will do if your expansion plans turn out to be a bad idea. In other words, never commit yourself to an irreversible expansion decision; always have a plan B since without it your company may not survive. Leave the backdoor open for a retreat in the event that the decision was wrong for whatever reason, like an economic downturn, faulty marketing analysis or stiff competition. This also applies to decisions regarding **vertical integration**, which will be discussed next.

I have spent most of my career either expanding or contracting companies as it has always been either feast or famine. In fact, I found it advantageous to move or relocate five of the six companies in my career for the purpose of either upsizing or downsizing. I also found it necessary to move one company to Mexico due to its labor-intensive operations in a highly competitive market. In our global economy it is not unusual for labor-intensive companies to follow the lower cost labor markets globally to Mexico, China, India and Viet Nam to mention just a few; you don't want to limit your options.

VERTICAL INTEGRATION

Companies sometimes decide to increase its profits by "vertically integrating" its operations. Vertical integration means that a company cuts out the middleman, so to speak, in an effort to maximize its profits by manufacturing component parts for its operations rather than buying them from a supplier. (Horizontal integration is simply the acquisition of a similar company.)

Vertical integration has the same downside as a company with a large economy of scale because it usually requires both a significant capital investment in equipment and higher fixed overhead costs in terms of facilities and management.

Unlike a larger economy of scale, however, vertical integration does not necessarily provide for an increase in the company's final product output.

What both a larger economy of scale and vertical integration have in common is that during the good times they will benefit the company with increased profitability, and during the bad times they will add to its losses.

Usually a large economy of scale and vertical integration will go hand-in-hand since smaller companies would be hard pressed to justify manufacturing its own component parts at its lower production levels. The exception is in manufacturing custom parts that are unique to your company's products.

Your ultimate decision whether or not to vertically integrate will be dependent on your analysis of the BEPT (Break Even Point) and the prospects of making a profit.

You must also weigh your level of acceptable risk of the possibility of losing both your capital investment and profits in the event of a business reversal. Unless the parts to be produced are of a low volume production nature, like unique custom parts, you will most likely find that trying to improve your profitability by essentially competing against a mass-producing parts supplier is simply not possible.

If you decide to manufacture your own parts, then you may want to consider operating under a different business name and compete against existing parts suppliers; however, this will most likely prove to be more difficult to justify due to the additional overhead costs of advertising and marketing, not to mention the costs of a sales department, shipping department, accounts receivable department and credit analyst. Additionally, the competitors of your primary business may be averse to purchasing its parts from a competitor's subsidiary.

As an example of a successful attempt to vertically integrate, a motor home manufacturer manufactured all of its major exterior fiberglass parts (front, rear and roof caps) in-house. This provided the company with a substantial parts cost savings, which in turn gave it an incredible pricing advantage over its competitors.

Since the company's products were price sensitive and also because it had a large economy of scale with excess production capacity, it used the cost savings to reduce the selling price of its products. This in turn increased its sales volume and profits.

Had the company's products not been price sensitive or had it not had excess production capacity, then it would have simply pocketed the cost savings as additional profits.

As an example of an unsuccessful attempt, during the early 1970's in the motor home manufacturing business a company decided to manufacturer its own laminated sidewalls. Each sidewall was composed of a composite sandwich wall construction of aluminum sheets bonded to a wood and staple wall structure. The company even trademarked the manufacturing process for its advertising and brochures as "Collateral Construction", which in retrospect should have been called "Collateral Damage". Even though it required an investment in large custom built vacuum machines, it was basically low-tech, so how difficult could it possibly be? The vacuum machines facilitated the bonding process of gluing the component parts together by using both heat and pressure applied uniformly over the entire sidewall.

Vacuum machines were nothing new, however, the company learned two valuable lessons the hard way. First, it learned that despite using heat in the laminating process, the quality of the structural integrity was extremely dependent on the ambient humidity level. Consequently, on high humidity days it had to refrain from operating the equipment. Secondly, and more importantly, after several years of operations it learned that the aluminum skin would react chemically under certain conditions with the steel staples used in constructing the wood sidewall structure. The chemical reaction was called "electrolysis", which is a corrosion process that takes place when two dissimilar metals (aluminum and steel) come into contact with each other under certain conditions involving moisture or condensation. The resulting damage to the sidewall was so prevalent within the industry that it actually had a name, "wall cancer". The repair costs and lawsuits were extremely costly nationwide. The initial production fix was to apply a special coating over the staples as a protective barrier between it and the aluminum siding. This eventually evolved into the ultimate solution of laminating flat sheets of fiberglass in lieu of aluminum.

Don't underestimate the learning curve of operating a new business in which you have no previous experience. **The best advice is to hire an expert who has the experience, as both start-up problems and unexpected technical problems can be disastrous.**

As an example of a successful attempt that was short lived, I was involved in a vertical integration at a motor home manufacturing company when we decided to start manufacturing our own furniture. Business had been extremely good in terms of volume, which justified our decision; however, five years later our business slowed down to the point that it was costing the company more to manufacture the furniture than to purchase it from a supplier. It was a double whammy as we were losing money in both our core business and in the manufacturing of the furniture.

Reversing directions was not that easy and was extremely expensive. Closing down the furniture business and liquidating the specialty equipment was only a small part of the cost. The greatest cost turned out to be in subleasing the building that we had acquired which was extremely difficult during the economic recession.

In our greed to maximize profits we lost sight of the "bad time cycle" which I had mentioned earlier as having happened every five to six years during my career. **Never forget that you need to plan for the bad times during the good times in order to survive.**

Michael Hill

WHEN YOUR COMPANY GETS SUED

While I am not an attorney and am not giving legal advise my experience has given me certain beliefs.

Avoid being sued if at all possible because once you have been sued, you have already lost, even if you eventually win the case. The reason is because of the high legal cost of defending yourself. You must be flexible and learn to be creative to resolve legal disputes; never get emotionally involved because of your negative feelings toward the plaintiff. Always keep to your core principles, but don't be so stubborn or emotionally entrenched that you are not willing to be flexible, as legal cases have a way of taking on a life of its own at a tremendous cost in both time and money.

Whenever our company was sued, for any reason, I would analyze the case and if I determined that we were not the proper or only responsible party in the lawsuit, then I would determine who else was a likely responsible party. Then, and only then, rather than filing a cross complaint against the likely responsible party or parties, I would contact the CEO's of those companies and explain the nature of the lawsuit and how our experts had determined that they were the most likely responsible party in the lawsuit.

I would then structure a multi party settlement to save everyone's legal fees. As an example, after being sued for $100,000, and after spending about $10,000 to answer the complaint along with our expert's analysis of the evidence, I contacted the plaintiff directly to see what it would take to settle the case without incurring any additional legal fees on either side. I then contacted the CEO's of the other two responsible parties to give them a heads-up of a cross complaint that we would be filing.

After discussing the case, including our findings, I explained my philosophy of how the legal costs make us all losers even if we ultimately win the case. With a settlement figure in hand, I shared that information and suggested a pragmatic approach to nip this lawsuit in the bud. In this particular case, the plaintiff was willing to settle for $70,000; so, I suggested that the three of us participate in a settlement offer. I told them that even though our company had already spent $10,000 that I was willing to propose an offer to the plaintiff; $60,000 and split the cost equally at $20,000 each. They agreed provided I could put it together as both CEO's thought that it would be a great outcome and applauded my efforts. The bottom line was that the case was settled for $66,000 with each of us participating equally at $22,000.

Despite an attorney advising me that this approach may be considered illegal due to it being considered "extortion", I learned that a pragmatic approach works very well and that the recipients always appreciated it since it was such a rational approach.

"Extortion" is basically a threat to do something against someone, like filing a lawsuit unless they give you something, like money. In my case I was prepared to file a cross complaint so I was simply giving them a courtesy call so as not to blindside them and by giving them a possible solution. In retrospect, the company's attorney would have recommended that I first file a complaint against them and then call with a possible solution. Unfortunately, this approach would have added to everyone's legal fees, which would have been contrary to my proposed solution of saving legal fees. If presented properly this approach should never be a problem. It is simply the reality of where we are and how it can be avoided.

I have used this approach a number of times and was successful every single time; and, without exception no one ever mentioned the word extortion, as they all thought my approach was simply a creative and pragmatic approach to a mutual problem. Since I am not a lawyer I was legally allowed to contact the plaintiff directly without going through their attorney. This would have only added to their cost and ultimately the cost of the settlement. There actually is an advantage to not being an attorney in the business world.

Here is an example of what not to do. I was handling a $50,000 lawsuit that could have been settled for a total of $35,000 ($25,000 to the plaintiff and $10,000 in legal fees). Another vice president (who else but Dick) refused to have me settle the case because he absolutely hated the plaintiff. Well, two and a half years later the case went to binding arbitration whereby the plaintiff received $35,000 but our legal fees amounted to a whopping $96,000 for a grand total of $131,000. The only one who was happy was our attorney. Whenever I think of this case it really upsets me in that the president didn't override the vice president's decision. I believe, however, that the president was intentionally going against his own better judgment in order to allow the other vice president to extract his pound of flesh, but we all know that a pound of flesh requires a lot of blood letting and in our case it was in the form of cash.

"An ounce of prevention is worth a pound of cure." Anonymous

CLASS ACTION LAWSUITS

At Rexhall Industries I learned how to negotiate a favorable settlement of a class action lawsuit. Despite having successfully handled negotiations of dozens of lawsuits, I was not prepared for a 5 million dollar "class action lawsuit". Unlike regular lawsuits, a class action lawsuit can't be simply negotiated and settled for a few bucks as a class action settlement requires the approval of a judge due to there being an unspecified number of plaintiffs. In order to file a class action lawsuit it requires at least three plaintiffs but it represents an entire class of unknown plaintiffs. Even though the plaintiffs' attorneys are required to look out for the best interest of his or her clients, I quickly realized that their primary objective was to make money. Knowing that simple fact armed me with a plan of action and I learned a valuable lesson of how to successfully handle these types of lawsuits in the future. The basis for the lawsuit was a claim of false advertising, which resulted in alleged damages to the plaintiffs by not receiving the full value of what they had expected to receive when they purchased the company's product.

The false advertising allegation was based on a trade magazine ad in which the company had continued to run its standard long running ad, which depicted a certain amount of steel members in its motor home sidewall construction. Even though there was no structural compromise, some steel had been removed from its sidewalls to facilitate its new model-year design. Due to its new laminated sidewall construction, the new design was actually stronger and weighed less than the old design; however, the company had failed to change its ads in a timely manner.

Since I knew that the attorneys were interested in cash, of which we had a limited amount, I needed to get settlement talks started immediately before the plaintiff's attorneys invested too much time, which would only cost more in legal fees. I proposed to settle this case in a manner in which the attorneys would get what they wanted, cash; and, they could also claim a victory for their clients without breaking the bank. Since their clients had purchased the company's product in the past, it occurred to me that they might be interested in a future purchase. I also realized that since there might be as many as 1,000 members in the class, it would be too costly to offer them cash, so I needed to offer them something tangible other than cash. Consequently, I proposed to pay for the attorney's legal fees and offer the class members a 2% rebate, or $1,000, on their next purchase of the company's products, as the average purchase price of the company's products was $50,000. If accepted, not only would the company have an opportunity to sell more of its products to its past customers, but also the company would add to its profits due to an increase in its future sales, not to mention the fact that the company could always build the 2% discount into its future product pricing. As it turned out, the lawsuit was settled on very favorable terms for the company.

Michael Hill

GOOD WORK HABITS

Anything worth doing is worth doing well; so, be consistent in your work habits and develop the discipline to be organized. I have found that being well organized is a great way to reduce your daily stress, which makes it easier to accomplish your tasks in a systematic manner. The discipline to develop good work habits requires three things; <u>knowing</u> how to accomplish what you want, having the <u>ability</u> to accomplish it, and the <u>desire</u> to want to do it regardless of how difficult. Being a procrastinator is very stressful, so an attitude of doing whatever it takes to accomplish a task from the get-go will not only make you more effective with less stress but will also impress your employer. Don't ever view your employment as just a job but rather as a career in which you have a passion for your work and a desire to succeed.

As an example of establishing a good work habit of working-out at the gym, you must <u>know</u> how to perform the exercises safely, the equipment that will be required and the best exercise program to attain your goal. You must also have the <u>ability</u> to perform the exercises safely and effectively, and you must have the <u>desire</u> to want to obtain your goal in order to justify your dedication of time and effort.

Good habits are easy to break; so, you should make it a lifelong goal to maintain those work habits. My wife, Lynne, told me a very impressive story about a high school track star who kept his dedication to his successful workout habits despite a broken leg, which sidelined him for six months. In order to keep his habit of getting up early to be at the track by 6 AM every day to get a work out in before the start of classes, he continued to arrive at the track at 6AM every day even though he couldn't run. He obviously knew that good habits are easy to break and it was not going to happen to him. He hated to get up that early, but he also knew how much he had to work to become a star and he was not going to give up what had made him successful.

"If you can't learn to do it well, learn to enjoy doing it badly." Anonymous

YES, WE ARE ALL PROCRASTINATORS

By listening to others and by learning from my own trials and errors I have discovered a valuable lesson that I believe can benefit everyone. Having the discipline to develop and maintain good work habits, like the story of the track star, will obviously serve you well but how do we do that? Well, the more difficult the task the greater the chances are that we will be a procrastinator even though we are generally not. Obviously, we do the things we like and don't do the things that we don't like. As an example, we all know that exercise can be very beneficial to our health but most of us hate to workout; so, very few will actually force themselves to develop the habit of working-out on a regular basis. We all know that New Year's resolutions usually don't last very long despite our best intentions. So why is that? Well, your success is inversely proportional to the level of its difficulty. In other words, the easier the task the greater your success rate, but the more difficult the task the less successful you will be. Since most "resolutions" are objectives that we have already tried before and failed, we are predisposed to fail again because our mind-set is that it is simply too difficult. If a task were made less difficult, our chances of success would be greater, right? Okay, this is obvious enough but how does this knowledge help. I wanted to get into the habit of working-out in the gym for an hour every other day. Even though the workouts were exhilarating, after a few weeks I found more than enough excuses to not workout for the rest of my life! My biggest excuse was that I was just too damn tired, period. Okay, maybe I will try it again next January. Yes, that ugly word "try" which we all know is not a real commitment.

A financial incentive should be an effective means of attaining our goal, at least that's what my good friends, Ken and Karen, thought. They told me that if they simply paid for a two-year gym membership that they would be obligated to go; but, after just one workout, they simply couldn't find the time. About a year later the urge to exercise returned, especially since they had already spent the money; so, they got their workout gear together and drove to the gym. Unfortunately, they couldn't find the gym.

After circling the block several times they realized that the building had been torn down and the gym was out of business! At least they didn't feel guilty about not working out!

I found that <u>the secret to success is to reduce the difficulty level</u> of your objectives to make them less daunting. I realized that just thinking about going to the gym was mentally exhausting. The more I failed to workout, the worse I felt; I would get a little depressed and even more tired which just reinforced my reason for not working out in the first place. I just saw it as a bad idea. How's that for a great excuse? And believe me, I had plenty more. In any event, the solution was actually a mental trick so that I would not feel badly about not working out. <u>I reduced the difficulty level of my objective; I promised myself that I would workout just 5 minutes every other day and only more if I felt like it, so an hour workout was now totally optional.</u> This is what I call a <u>no guilt, no failure commitment</u>. How big of a loser would I be if I couldn't keep this easy commitment? Well, there are two things that I already knew: one, I always felt great both physically and mentally after an hour workout; two, and more importantly, I knew that once I started working-out, regardless of how tired I felt beforehand, both the blood flow and the endorphins would kick in and I would want to continue my workout for an entire hour. I ended up working-out for an hour at least 9 out of 10 times, even if I had a slight headache before hand. This <u>no guilt, no failure</u> workout has been working great for me for over 13 years now and counting.

As a cautionary note, I have found it necessary over the years to <u>continually remind myself that it will just be a 5-minute workout</u> as it will always be an ongoing process because it is simply way too easy to fail, especially as one gets older.

I have also applied this philosophy to other chores like cleaning all of the windows in my house, which like most people I really hate. If you think about cleaning all of the windows in your house, you will never get around to it. If you set a goal of just cleaning a few windows today, then you will find that once you get all of your supplies ready and get started you will end up doing more. <u>Just get started and don't overwhelm yourself with the magnitude of the entire task.</u>

"A journey of a thousand miles starts with a single step" Lao-Tzu

"Never put off till tomorrow what you can do the day after tomorrow." Mark Twain

"I always wanted to be a procrastinator, but I never got around to it!" Anonymous

HOW TO DEAL WITH NEGATIVE TALK

You can't control what may or may not be said about you so don't get caught up in petty comments. Keep in mind that you really don't know what you are being told was really said about you or not. Also, the messenger is not always acting in your best interest. In fact, some are simply playing the dangerous game of politics. They will try to either ingratiate themselves to you or pit you against another employee with whom they do not like or who is standing in their way for a promotion. By exhibiting a cavalier attitude toward what they are telling you, you will also send the appropriate message to the messenger as well.

Some people will try to undermine your confidence by stabbing you in the back; just nip it in the bud by saying, "What people say about me behind my back is none of my business." This sends the message that you are secure and confident in your abilities. Rumors and gossip go both ways; so, when your attitude about what you were told gets back to the offending party, it will help discourage efforts to discredit you in the future.

"What people say about me behind my back is none of my business." Ru Paul

"I don't at all like knowing what people say of me behind my back. It makes me far too conceited." Oscar Wilde

SALARIED VERSUS HOURLY EMPLOYEES

By law, hourly employees receive time and a half pay for working over 8 hours per day or over 40 hours per week. Most salaried employees are exempt from this rule, so when hourly employees become an exempt salaried employee, their mindset and work habits must be changed from the get-go. Don't assume that someone who has been an hourly employee for most of their working life will understand exactly what is expected of him or her with respect to the number of hours that will be required in a new capacity.

Most will feel at first that they still have an 8 to 5 job with an hour for lunch with the added benefit of being able to miss some time off work without having their pay docked. It must be made clear from the get-go that they are salaried employees and are exempt from overtime pay and, even though most of the time they will be required to work regular business hours, they must do whatever it takes to get the job done, which may require 12 hour days and even working weekends on occasion.

Unfortunately, most former hourly employees have a clock in their head that tells them that for every hour of work over 40 hours per week the company owes them additional pay or an equal amount of time off. This is a totally unacceptable mindset, so I always tell new salaried employees that their salary is based on working an average of 45 hours per week. If they find that they are consistently working an average of more than that, I will determine the reason and take appropriate action as employees may get burned out or develop a negative attitude. I may discover that the employee is either not well organized or simply incapable of doing the job. If this is not the case, I may reduce his or her workload by shifting it to another department, consider getting them additional help, or reward them. A reward for their extra effort and dedication to the company could mean a raise, a special bonus, or consideration for a promotion.

IF YOU WANT SOMEONE TO BE YOUR FRIEND, THEN LET THEM DO YOU A FAVOR.

I could not help but include this old saying which my mother taught me because it seems so strange and counter intuitive, but I have learned that it is very true. "If you want someone to be your friend, then let them do you a favor". If people generally like you, then most will be genuinely pleased that you are asking them for help because they are often flattered that you recognize their expertise and that you trust them to help you. In fact, some will even go to extraordinary lengths to impress you. This often leads to a closer relationship, especially if there is something that you can do for them in return without them asking as a sign of your appreciation.

IF YOU WANT SOMETHING DONE, GIVE IT TO A BUSY PERSON

This too seems a little strange and even counter intuitive but "If you want something to get done, then give it to a busy person". This saying, which my mother also taught me, I found to be true. Busy people are generally the best employees in the workplace; they are never at rest because they are self-starters. After they complete a project they move on to the next one, or find something productive to do, even if it is just cleaning up their work area. Those who always have time on their hands, more often than not, are just trying to do the minimum to get by. Due to poor work habits, they tend to be procrastinators. You will often hear from them that they simply can't handle any more work. If you assign a project to these people you will often hear the dreaded "I'll try" and that means they will usually disappoint you.

We have all heard of self-starters, the self motivated over-achievers, but we don't hear about the bottom 10 to 25% of employees, whom I call "self-stoppers". These people consume a lot of our time in follow-ups, are under-achievers and unfortunately every company has them. Jack Welch, a previous CEO for General Electric, had a unique solution to this problem: he would fire the bottom 10% each and every year like clockwork!

As previously stated, I believe in making sure that employees know where they stand and if they are not meeting the company's standards then they are given ample opportunity to correct their deficiencies. I do not subscribe to turning over 10%, or any percentage for that matter of the employees every year because I believe it denigrates your employee's number one priority; namely, job security.

PUTTING YOUR BEST FOOT FORWARD

People like to deal with people whom they like, or who have made a good impression. First impressions set the tone for the future since most people are very quick to qualify others as likeable and trustworthy, or not. On the other hand, you should not be too quick to qualify or judge others, unless you are an excellent judge of character which most of us are not.

It is not easy to remember people's names, especially if you are meeting a number of people for the first time. However, if you do, you will make a great first impression. Making a point of using someone's name during the course of a meeting helps reinforce their name in your mind, but more intensive efforts may be dictated by the situation. Remembering someone's name is a very personal thing, which shows that you feel that they are important enough for you to remember their name. The more people who you are introduced to at a meeting, the more impact of your remembering their names will have on them. I learned how impressive this is from Cindy Costner (Kevin Costner's ex-wife) who is excellent at remembering names. My wife and I were one of 20 couples in the neighborhood that Ms. Costner had invited to view her house. She had torn down a 5,000 square foot ranch style house across the street and built a beautiful 8,500 square foot French country house. There were no nametags, but upon leaving her house, she addressed everyone by their first name. We were extremely impressed, especially since we spent very little time actually talking with her during our visit, yet she still found it important enough to remember our names! Obviously, she has a great ability for remembering names but I am sure that it does not come without some effort.

Consequently, two weeks prior to starting work at a new job as a vice president, I asked the president for a personnel list so that I could commit the names of 30 employees to memory in an effort to hit the ground running on my first day. I felt that it would be invaluable to me and it was exactly that. Once I had the names memorized, all I had to do was to put a face with each name. I probably spent a half-hour a day for two weeks reading over the list of 30 names before I felt I was ready. It worked like a charm, especially since I was not only genuinely excited about meeting these people, but I could finally assign a name to each face. If you are entering a company, especially as a top executive, you certainly don't want people to feel like you don't value them enough to even remember their name.

"We only get one chance to make a good first impression."
Anonymous

LEARN TO LOVE YOUR JOB

Generally speaking, work is not fun, but it can be. In fact, it is not difficult to make a game out of everything that you do, like getting a task done by noon or done faster than the last time. By making everything a game, you are constantly challenging yourself to win because <u>you now have a vested interest in the outcome</u>. I like to think that an analogous situation is the increased interest that one has in watching a sporting event after making a wager, which otherwise they would have absolutely zero interest in watching. Since you know that you have to do the work anyway, you might as well make it a game and have fun with it. This may sound silly, but I have learned that it really works. Your reward for accomplishing a task is the satisfaction of getting it done, getting it done quickly and the spare time that you will have to perform other more complex duties in a more relaxed mood without the pressures of time related stress.

The effective leader will also utilize this strategy with his or her subordinates to engender enthusiasm that will result in a substantial improvement in both morale and efficiency. An offer of a free lunch or some other token of appreciation for "winning" is always helpful in reinforcing a team spirit. Who doesn't want to be a winner?

Be realistic in your estimated time to perform a task or a series of tasks, as you want a challenge, but don't want to set yourself up for failure.

Always be goal oriented and set a goal for everything that you want to accomplish. This process will also make you acutely aware of time and your ability to perform efficiently. The busier you become the more aware you will be of your time consciousness as everything that you do is a function of time. Over the course of time you will become a great estimator of the time it takes to perform tasks, even those that you have never performed before. This will be a tremendous help in scheduling both your time and your priorities. This will also aid you in scheduling the length of meetings based on your knowledge of the topics and your feel for the amount of time each person will need to express their point of view.

"If work was suppose to be fun, then why do all of the rich people let the rest of us do it?" Anonymous

NEVER PRESENT PROBLEMS WITHOUT SOLUTIONS

Your boss is where the proverbial buck stops, so it is natural to give him or her the problems that you are not certain how to resolve; however, nobody has a corner on good ideas, so make it a habit to present possible solutions for every problem that you pass on to your boss. Without even having to ask you for your suggestions your boss will be very impressed to have the benefit of not only your perception of the problem, but also possible solutions. This approach will gain you equity with your boss and will hopefully show that you are a capable and concerned problem solver who is deserving of more responsibility and a possible promotion when the time is right. Sadly enough, I have rarely seen employees offer possible solutions as most seem satisfied to wash their hands of the problem and move on. Consequently, this approach will absolutely set you apart from the pack, and trust me it will always be appreciated.

My mechanic told me, "I couldn't repair your brakes, so I made your horn louder." Steven Wright

BEFORE YOU FIRE THEM, GIVE THEM A RAISE

"When you have employees not living up to the company's expectations; then, when all else fails, give them a raise before you fire them!" I thought that this was very strange when Tom Frank, the President of Executive Industries, told me this as a 27 year-old Vice President in charge of 1,100 employees. I thought that he was joking; I had never heard this before. He went on to say that when you find that it is impossible to motivate someone, then as a last resort, see if a raise will change their attitude and work habits. If this fails then you must fire them quickly as you would not want to send the wrong message to other employees (you may also get less employees clamoring for raises).

I learned that by giving them a raise you not only get their undivided attention for constructive criticism; but, possibly, their poor performance is because they feel that they are underpaid. Giving them a raise usually results in a more receptive mood affording you one last opportunity to explain what you expect of them and why you feel they are failing. As an additional benefit, they will now be putting a higher paying job at risk and just maybe they will value it enough to make corrective changes. I found that this worked only about 50% of the time but being able to retain that 50% was well worth it.

DON'T TAKE "NO" FOR AN ANSWER

Fortunately, I did not have to overcome a "no" until after I had graduated with an undergraduate degree from USC. With a B.S. degree and good grades in engineering classes, I was readily accepted into the USC Graduate School of Engineering. Unfortunately, despite being really excited about enrolling in the Graduate School of Business, I received a rejection letter based on my average GRE (Graduate Records Exam) and a "B" undergraduate GPA.

Determined to get into the graduate business program, I made an appointment with the Dean of Business. I first asked him if it would be possible to reconsider his rejection letter as I wanted to see how entrenched he was in his decision. He said, "Mike, let me put it this way, the reason would have to be very compelling as we have rejected nearly 20% of all applicants with many being more qualified than you." Well, that was good news. No, I'm not kidding because at least now I knew that there was a possibility despite the bar being set really high.

I argued that standard testing didn't account for dedication and hard work. I also pointed out that a "B" GPA in a BS program should be weighed somewhat higher than the same average in a BA program. He somewhat agreed with a slight nod but said, "There are still more qualified applicants on the waiting list".

What waiting list? He hadn't said anything about a damn waiting list but it obviously was a list of applicants who had qualified, but who were not admitted due to the school being full.

My objective was not to be on a waiting list, so I told him how I had worked my way through school by operating my own business and had still graduated in four years. At this point I could see that I was starting to get his full attention. Not wanting to lose any momentum, I then proceeded to explain how, for the first time, I would no longer be working 20 hours per week while taking a full class load since I had just sold my company and would be able to devote 100% of my efforts towards my studies. I will never forget what happened next. He stood up, reached across his desk to shake my hand and said, "Mike, welcome to the Graduate School of Business".

Not having to work while attending school was really a blessing as I now had time to burn; so, I decided to pursue both the engineering and business graduate programs simultaneously. I have never told this story to anyone before, other than to my parents, as I have always felt a little embarrassed that I had not been accepted outright, but rather had to talk my way in. In retrospect, however, I am very proud that I did not accept "no" for an answer.

Interestingly enough, the Dean said that to my credit I was the only one who had asked to speak with him regarding his rejection letter. Surprisingly, everyone else had accepted "no" for an answer, so in his mind, just requesting a meeting gave me a leg up! I thanked him and said that I would not let him down for having faith in me; and I am proud to say that I didn't. In fact, my commitment to him motivated me even more as letting people down has never been something that I have ever taken lightly.

There is another lesson here. If you want to lose weight, stop smoking, or start exercising, then let others know of your goal. It will then be more difficult to not accomplish your goal since no one wants to look like a loser, especially to those whom you respect and who have faith in you.

Michael Hill

ALWAYS HAVE A "PLAN B"

At Executive Industries I worked with John Summers, General Manager of GM's recreational truck chassis division, on a concept chassis design our company had converted from a GM chassis. Essentially we converted a front engine GM truck chassis to a rear engine chassis. The advantage of this conversion was that it made the driver's compartment much quieter, it eliminated the large motor box cover which made it easier to get in and out of the driver's and passenger's seats, and the reduction of about 2,000 pounds off of the front axle gave a superior ride, as most front engine models were very close to the maximum front axle rating and rode like a large lumber truck in comparison. This was a secret project that I had not shared with John until the prototype had been completed and thoroughly tested. Our sales force was chomping at the bit to have it put into production but we had a major hurdle ahead of us, which would make or break the successful launch of this product. The question was, "Would GM stand behind their warranty for such a highly modified chassis?" If not, then the retail buyers would balk and not purchase our vehicle.

Well, John became a great ally because he was really impressed with what we had accomplished. In fact, he said that he had attempted to get GM to do exactly what we had done years earlier but was rejected due to concerns about the limited size of the market. Consequently, he wanted to approve our chassis for warranty coverage but told me there was no way in hell that he could approve warranty coverage for such a highly modified chassis. Since I was prepared for an outright rejection, I immediately suggested that we reach a compromise position whereby GM would stand behind their warranty and in turn Executive would reimburse GM for any warranty costs associated with its chassis modifications. John said that he really wanted us to succeed and also wanted to see it hit the market prior to his retirement, so he approved it in writing. This product turned out to be a great hit and helped Executive achieve the coveted number one selling luxury motor home in 1984 (according to the R.L. Polk retail registration report). It was a calculated risk, but it paid off in a big way and helped propel the company to profitability for the first time in four years.

I learned that the best way to have a proposal accepted was to be prepared with a fallback position of another proposal. In fact, the greater the number of fallback positions, the better your chances, so always be prepared to be flexible.

"The most successful people are those who are good at plan B." James York

"THERE IS NO LIMIT TO HOW FAR YOU CAN GO, AS LONG AS YOU DON'T CARE WHO GETS THE CREDIT"
President Harry Truman

This quote, from President Harry Truman, is very true. Always give credit where credit is due and never be afraid to give more credit than you take. No one likes someone who hogs all of the credit. Our egos naturally demand that we receive credit when we feel that it is deserved but fight this impulse, as it simply does nothing to further your cause and can really hurt you. Giving credit to others will be respected and will make people more likely to help you in the future, as they will know that you are not a glory hog. Always remember that, in the end, all fair-minded people will know the true importance of your contribution, so simply be confident in your own feeling of self-worth regardless of whether it is acknowledged or not.

USING E-MAILS AS A GREAT TOOL

I have learned that e-mails are great for both communicating and memorializing the communications. They are better than a phone call because you don't interrupt anyone, and the e-mail can be read when the recipients have the time and interest without interruptions. In fact, if need be, they can read it a number of times to make sure that they clearly understand it.

You should make a hard copy and set up a tickler file for the purpose of following up in the event that a response is not received within a reasonable amount of time, or preferably a specified time. Always make sure that you communicate a time when you expect to receive a response.

Make sure to address one person at a time. I have seen a number of e-mails addressed to three people that is asking for something to get done but it is not clear which one of the three is being held responsible. The sender is assuming that the responsible party will understand that the e-mail is directed to him or her, and that the others were simply listed as an F.Y.I., but falls into the trap of later finding out that the "responsible party" did not recognize this. Instead, send c.c.'s to the other parties.

Recognize that whatever you say in e-mails will be forever memorialized. Think carefully about what you say because lawyers love it when you don't

KNOW WHEN TO SHUT UP

I am amazed at how many times I have witnessed someone who continues to talk in negotiations, or depositions, when it would have served them better to just shut up. Sometimes it is best not to correct someone who has said something that is not true when you know better. It is not a lie to remain silent and allow others to make their own mistakes, so <u>always think before you speak</u>.

Once in high school, my freshman English class was given an assignment to write a book report on any book of our choosing. Well, after reading the book of my choice, I realized that the author's summary on the inside cover was extremely comprehensive and better than anything that I was capable of writing; so, you guessed it, I simply copied it word for word and submitted it. I knew that the teacher would not have read this particular book and I was correct; however, unbeknownst to me at the time, a fellow student had read it and had submitted for his report the author's summary as well (I guess it is true that great minds really do think alike)!

Two weeks later the teacher walked through the classroom while placing each book report face down on our desks. When I turned mine over, I was shocked to see a red "F" at the top of the page! Of course my first thought was that the teacher didn't think that the author whom I had plagiarized was a very good writer. Keep in mind that this was the thinking of a 14 year old with less than a fully developed brain. Well, to my surprise the teacher asked me and a fellow student to stand and then proceeded to read my report paragraph by paragraph while alternately reading the other student's report. To everyone's amazement both reports were absolutely identical! While still standing, the teacher proceeded to say, " This was absolutely no accident and the two of you actually thought that you could get away with a two for one effort?" Even though that was not the case, our silence found us guilty of this lesser charge. As we both stood there, red faced and looking at each other, I am sure that we were thinking the same thing. How could anyone think that we were so stupid as to have worked together and then to have submitted two reports without changing a single word? In retrospect I believe that this was a new twist to the meaning of the saying, "It is best to have them think you a fool, than to speak and remove all doubt." In any event, I learned when it was best to just shut up.

While still a teenager I received a traffic ticket for "speed exhibition", essentially drag racing on a public street. Because of the severity of this offense, it was mandatory to appear in court even if you were not going to contest the ticket. I figured that they were going to make me an example by throwing the book at me and I knew that it was not going to go as well as the book report fiasco. Well, while standing before the judge, I could see that he was quickly perusing my ticket as he began to speak. In a very authoritarian tone of voice, he addressed the crowded courtroom and said, "Before me stands a young man who was caught speeding, going 50 mph in a 35 mph zone!" He then paused for the benefit of this outrageous fact to sink in, and then he said, "But the worst part is that this young man", okay here it comes, "actually was going 50 mph on wet streets after it had rained earlier in the day, which the officer noted here on the ticket!" Then there was a long silence and he finally addressed me directly and said, "What do you have to say for yourself?" Well, I pleaded guilty as charged, paid the fine and got out of Dodge as fast as I could.

"To steal ideas from one person is plagiarism; to steal from many is research." Steven Wright

GET A GUARANTEE OF PERFORMANCE

While working in Arkansas at the Ben Pearson Archery facility (owned by The Leisure Group) I walked by a boarded-up building on a daily basis. I was curious as to what was in the building and why it was necessary for both the doors and the windows to be boarded up, however, everyone that I asked refused to tell me. I was so busy working that I didn't press the issue but you might imagine the thoughts of some horror movie flashing through my mind.

After months of wondering who or what was buried in that building and wondering if one should be worried if it got out, I finally got a break from another executive who swore me to secrecy. He told me that the "Master Fletcher" was in the building! My first response was "Who is this Master Fletcher and is he dead or alive?" I figured that he had to be dead, as I had never seen anyone taking food into the building. After a good laugh he told me that it had cost the company $200,000 in 1970 dollars to automate the fletching process, which is the labor-intensive process of gluing feathers onto wood shafts to make arrows, hence the name Master Fletcher.

The embarrassment stemmed from the fact that it did not work and the company that had manufactured it told them, "For another $100,000, we will make it work!" I was happy to have this mystery solved; since now I understood why it was a top-secret as there had obviously been no guarantee in the contract that it would work. Someone very high up in the company screwed up big time, and probably decided that the embarrassment would simply go away if it was buried in a building and hushed up. Mystery solved.

"The only mystery in life is why the Kamikaze pilots wore helmets." Al McGuire

If you would like another example of how costly a lack of a guarantee can be, you need look no further than to the Affordable Health Care bill, a.k.a. Obamacare, and its disastrous computer roll out debacle in October 2013. The computer system cost over $600,000,000 with absolutely no guarantee that it would work and the cost to fix it was estimated to be an additional $300,000,000 with still no guarantees!

DON'T KICK THE TIRES TOO HARD

A polite respectful style of negotiating is critical when negotiating to buy something that the seller has emotional ties. The most expensive asset that most of us will ever purchase in our lifetime will be a house. Regardless of the cost, almost everyone takes great pride in his or her home. As in any negotiations, it will always be beneficial to know if there is an emotional attachment to the item that is being sold. Consequently, when buying a house, especially in a competitive market, you must be sensitive to the seller's feelings due to their emotional attachment.

As an example, in 1977 I was interested in purchasing a house that Vincent Bugliosi (the prosecutor in the Charles Manson case) was also interested in purchasing. Fortunately, my real estate broker informed me that she had heard that Bugliosi was kicking the tires pretty hard in an effort to get a better price, and the homeowners were a little put off by his negotiating tactics. I didn't know what he had offered, but it was obvious he was not offering the full asking price. I also knew that I would not win in a bidding war against him; so I felt that I had to make it known that my offer was going to be my final best offer. Since I didn't feel comfortable in offering the full asking price, I submitted an offer attached to a personal note. My note read, "I love everything that you have done to your home and feel that it is worth every cent that you are asking; however, the most that I can offer is X dollars, so it is my wish that you will find it acceptable." To my pleasant surprise they accepted my offer and we have been living in our house for 37 years now and counting. Instead of simply submitting an offer, my knowledge of my competitor's negative tactics gave me a decisive edge, which I was able to exploit.

EPILOGUE

Michael Hill

The importance of establishing a good reputation by embracing all of the principles enumerated in the second chapter can't be over emphasized. Of all of the turnaround companies in my career, none would have survived had it not been for the cooperation of hundreds of creditors who had to be sold, not only on the reorganization plan, but also, and more importantly, on the integrity of the management team.

Trusting others is a nice attribute, but always remember, <u>control is better than confidence</u>. Never put yourself in a position where you are not in control as your trust in others may not be as well founded as you think; you must do your own due diligence.

Be true to yourself by keeping your word and by admitting your own mistakes. Be honest not only with others but also with yourself as self-denial is self-destructive.

Always consider how a job-change will be reflected on your resume and how that will affect your career; don't jump from job to job.

You will be confronted by a number of situations in your career and the resulting first hand experiences, whether good or bad outcomes, will make you wiser.

Harboring hatred or resentment only harms you, so get over it as soon as possible and move on with your life because as Nelson Mandela put it, **"Resentment is like drinking poison and hoping it will kill your enemies."**

Always remember that **"happiness is just a state of mind"**, which money can't buy, and as Dale Carnegie put it, **"Success is getting what you want. Happiness is wanting what you get."**

Instead of "reinventing the wheel", learn as much as possible from those who have preceded you. Benefitting from other's successes and failures will position you well for success.

Since <u>knowledge is power</u>, get the best education possible and make sure that it includes accounting classes to better understand financial numbers. My mother often said, "You may have financial setbacks in your life and you may even lose everything in a bankruptcy, but the one thing that can't be taken away from you is your education." There is no better security in life than a good education; it will open doors that would otherwise be closed. Listening to her stories about the suffering with the high unemployment during the Great Depression of the 1930's and taking her advice regarding a good education has served me well.

Don't be afraid to experiment with new ideas despite setbacks as being creative and thinking outside the box is the best way to excel in business.

Surrounding yourself with team players that complement your own expertise is a great way to not only survive, but to thrive.

In closing I will leave you with one of the first and the very last piece of advice from my mother. When I was about 10 she told me that whatever I decided to do in my life I should strive to be the best at it even if I decided to be a garbage man. By striving to be the best I would become passionate and consequently proud, successful and happy. She went on to say that even if I was not as financially successful as others, it wouldn't matter since the satisfaction of knowing that I had done my very best is what would. In her words, "Be the best damn garbage man that you can possibly be." It certainly sounded a little strange to me at the time; **but it gave me a lasting attitude that I could never fail in life regardless of the level of financial rewards as long as I applied myself to the fullest.**

Her last piece of advice was from her death bed when she said, "Mike, never get old." In the context of our conversation about her failing health at age 79, she was encouraging me to continue to live a healthy life style. She had lived a healthy life style; however, cancer, M.S. and severe osteoporosis challenged her since the age of 40, yet she never complained. My father would often refer to her as Saint Jane. She truly was a great mentor and inspiration in my life.

Lastly, but certainly not least, I want to **thank you** for reading my book, and it is my hope that it helps you to live a happier and more prosperous life. If you are anything like me, then you will find it helpful to reread sections of this book, especially the one that defines happiness, **because happiness is what everyone should have as their life's goal, regardless of financial wealth.**

About The Author

Mike and his wife, Lynne, love all dogs, but their dog of choice is the Rottweiler, whom they love dearly and have raised for over 23 years.

He is an avid reader and especially enjoys books about the mysteries surrounding the technologies of ancient civilizations. He once read 25 books on the subject over a six-month period.

He also loves challenges, especially designing structures, which he then engineers and builds as a "hands on" contractor.

Having equipped an 800 square foot home gym, he shares his passion for working-out with his daughter, Audrey, an excellent self-employed personal trainer.

In retirement he is looking forward to spending quality time with his wife and three grandchildren, and, of course, enjoying USC football games.

As a Student at USC:
Bachelors of Science Degree in Industrial Engineering
Masters of Science Degree in Operations Research Engineering
Masters of Science Degree in Management Science
Member of Beta Gamma Sigma (Business school's Phi Beta Kappa.)
Member of Sigma Alpha Epsilon fraternity, Cal Gamma Chapter

As an Executive:
Vice President of Operations/CFO and Director of Krystal
Vice President/CFO and Director of Rexhall Industries
President/CEO and Director of Executive Industries
President/COO and Director of Apollo Motor Homes
Vice President of Operations of Vogue Coach
Vice President of Operations of Executive Industries
Project Manager of The Leisure Group
Owner of MTC Corporation and Better Products Company

Lightning Source UK Ltd.
Milton Keynes UK
UKHW010642060621
384992UK00001B/28